THE GIFT OF THE WORLD

THE GIFT
OF THE WORLD

*An Introduction to the
Theology of Dumitru Stăniloae*

CHARLES MILLER

T&T CLARK
EDINBURGH

T&T CLARK LTD
59 GEORGE STREET
EDINBURGH EH2 2LQ
SCOTLAND

First published 2000

ISBN 0 567 08696 8 HB
ISBN 0 567 08732 8 PB

British Library Cataloguing-in-Publication Data
A catalogue record for this book is available from the British Library

Typeset by Waverley Typesetters, Galashiels
Printed and bound in Great Britain by Bookcraft Ltd, Avon

For Donald

Contents

Acknowledgements

Most of the essays which constitute this book were originally delivered as lectures at the St. Theosevia Centre for Christian Spirituality, Oxford. The first three were given in 1987 at a day conference devoted to the thought of Dumitru Stăniloae. I am indebted to Fr. Robert Barringer, who was in Oxford prior to that occasion working on his English translation of the *Orthodox Dogmatic Theology*, for comments on the texts of those lectures. His knowledge of Fr. Stăniloae's thought is far wider than my own. The last chapter was also given as a lecture at the Centre in 1991 in conjunction with the Rt. Revd. Rowan Williams and the Rt. Revd. Kallistos Ware who spoke on other aspects of Fr. Stăniloae's thought. I am indebted to Canon A. M. Allchin, Director of the St. Theosevia Centre, for the encouragement to assemble the lectures in book form and, indeed, for first introducing me to Dumitru Stăniloae's writings in 1980 when I was a student at Nashotah House Theological Seminary. In addition, I wish to thank Dr. Dan-Ilie Ciobotea, now Metropolitan Daniel of Moldavia and Bucovinia, for his friendship and stimulating remarks about Fr. Stăniloae's writings; Fr. Christopher Newlands, the Anglican Chaplain in Bucharest, for his hospitality during a visit to Bucharest in 1993, and Mother Nazaria Niţa and her sisters of the Monastery of Văratic where I was lovingly cared for; and Fr. Alexander Popescu for his stimulating conversations about intellectual currents in Romania in this century.

ix

The preparation of this manuscript for publication would not have been possible without the generous efforts of Mrs. Mary Jenkins in England and Mrs. Sherri Kuehn and Mr. Jonathan Rowe in the United States.

Finally, I wish to thank my wife, Judith, for her support at every stage of research and writing.

Bishopstead
The Feast of All Saints, 1998

Introduction

It is a great moment when a monumental theological work becomes available to the wider church. Since its publication in 1978 Orthodox archpriest Dumitru Stăniloae's three-volume *Orthodox Dogmatic Theology* has until recently been available only to Romanian readers.[1] In 1985 installments began to appear in the French 'Théophanie' series, and a German translation of the *Dogmatic Theology* now complements the growing corpus of articles by Fr. Stăniloae himself and secondary literature about his thought among western Europeans.[2]

English-speaking readers have, by contrast, had access to a very small portion of Stăniloae's writings.[3] But with the first volume of a fully edited critical English edition of his *Orthodox Dogmatic Theology* now published in the United States under

---

[1] *Teologia Dogmatică Ortodoxă*, 3 vols. (Bucureşti, 1978). Henceforth cited as *DT* followed by volume and page.

[2] Two volumes in French comprising the first volume of the Romanian edition, entitled *Le génie de l'Orthodoxie* (Paris, 1985) and *Prière de Jésus et expérience du Saint-Esprit* (Paris, 1981); in German translation by H. Pitters, *Orthodoxe Dogmatik* (Zurich, Gütersloh: Berzinger, Gerd Mohn, 1985). From the secondary literature, comprising a French translation of four articles by Fr. Stăniloae on the divine attributes, is *Dieu est Amour*, trans. Daniel Neeser (Genève, 1980).

[3] See the select bibliography of publications in English, pp. 117–119.

the title *The Experience of God*, British and North American theologians, churchmen and scholars will have access to his *chef d'oeuvre*, the crown of a half-century of pioneering theological reflection.[4] There is no doubt that the failure to publish an English edition of his *Dogmatic Theology* in Fr. Stăniloae's lifetime was a cause of frustration since it deprived him of the chance for sustained and critical dialogue with English-speaking theologians such as access to the theological text alone affords.

The deprivation has been ours as well, however. In our ignorance of Stăniloae's writings we have lacked the insights of a man whose theological stature has been compared to that of Barth, Tillich, Rahner and Schillebeeckx.[5] Indeed, Stăniloae's *Dogmatic Theology* is a uniquely systematic articulation of Christian faith by one of Orthodoxy's most creative voices. But in Dumitru Stăniloae we meet not only a great contemporary *Orthodox* theologian but a Christian thinker of truly ecumenical proportions.[6] Olivier Clément has rightly insisted, I think, that Stăniloae's perspective is not just 'ecumenical' but 'catholic' – it is total and all-embracing.[7]

Although the circumstances of the Romanian Orthodox Church prior to the revolution of 1989 prevented full circulation and discussion of Stăniloae's ideas both in his own country and in the West, it may be providential that access to his *Orthodox Dogmatic Theology* is beginning only now. In contrast to previous decades when the very notion of dogmatic theology was largely *passé* and theological specialisms, often with extremely limited concerns, were in the ascendancy, we now seem to be entering a period of theological consolidation. The ground swell changes in the tone, shape, language and content of theology over the past thirty years are bearing fruit in major syntheses.

[4] Dumitru Stăniloae, *The Experience of God*, trans. and ed, Ioan Ioniță and Robert Barringer (Brookline, 1994).

[5] His significance is estimated thus by Ion Bria, 'The Creative Vision of D. Stăniloae: an Introduction to his Theological Thought,' *The Ecumenical Review*, 33, no. 1 (January, 1981): 53.

[6] So Dan-Ilie Ciobotea, 'Une dogmatique de l'homme d'aujourd'hui,' *Irénikon*, 54, no. 4 (1981): 472–474.

[7] Olivier Clément in his *Préface* to *Le génie de l'Orthodoxie*, p. 21.

The appearance in English of Hans Urs von Balthasar's massive *The Glory of the Lord*, of Jürgen Moltmann's major studies, ending most recently with *The Spirit of Life*, and Wolfhart Pannenberg's *Systematic Theology* testify that from the Roman Catholic, Reformed and Lutheran sides respectively, systematic – we might even say dogmatic – theology is alive and well. So the time is right for the appearance of a comparable contribution from the rich tradition of Orthodoxy, one which is consciously free from the scholastic constraints of the Orthodox past and open to the needs, concerns, values and aspirations of Christians living in an industrial and technological age.

This small volume of essays is offered as a kind of prolegomenon to the *Orthodox Dogmatic Theology*. I do so in the awareness that for the majority of students of theology, especially in the English-speaking world, Stăniloae and his theological vision are an unknown quantity. Yet his *Orthodox Dogmatic Theology* will be read and studied only to the degree that the theological world knows its potential riches. The wide thematic scope of even the first volume of the *Dogmatic Theology* cannot be comprehended in the relatively brief chapters of this book; nor have I tried specifically to treat the four 'master-themes' which Bishop Kallistos Ware has highlighted in his admirable 'Foreword' to *The Experience of God*.[8] Instead, I wish to go behind those particular concerns to take up a pervasive theme which, while deeply rooted in Stăniloae's dogmatic and systematic treatments, lies beneath them like a persistent, rich melodic line. While rooted in a creative application of Orthodoxy's rich patristic and Byzantine heritage, it connects too with Stăniloae's own personal sensibilities and acts as a key point of contact with his ascetical, sacramental and – for lack of a better word – existential concerns. I mean Fr. Stăniloae's theme of gift; his view of the creation and created existence as the primordial gift of God. Like the distinctive brush-stroke of a great artist it reappears again and again and unifies Fr. Dumitru's diverse intellectual and spiritual universe.

To claim that this book introduces its reader to the *Orthodox Dogmatic Theology* as a whole or to its first English volume, *The*

---

[8] *Experience*, pp. xix–xxv.

Experience of God, is not wholly accurate therefore. Rather, it seeks to give the reader a taste of Stăniloae's deeply integrated approach to the Good News by exploring one of his most distinctive and all-embracing themes.

I believe too that such a presentation is timely. At various levels and in different ways the theme of creation has come to the fore. 'Green theology' is more and more prevalent, with its desire to give a viable theological meaning to our planet's faltering environment. The growing sense of ecological crisis has given rise to what some have called creation-centred spirituality which eagerly encourages Christians to celebrate creation and to overcome the alleged dualism in the Christian mindset.[9] In North America, at least, Matthew Fox has become its guru. However curious some of his ideas and language may be from the point of view of orthodox Christianity, Fox's fundamental desire to reclaim an 'earthly' Christianity and to construct a meaningful Christian cosmology are not to be wholly dismissed.[10] From within the Orthodox tradition itself Philip Sherrard has raised the alarm against the 'industrial and technological inferno' which we have created. In his introduction to a recent book on this theme Sherrard described the problem thus:

> . . . the crisis itself is not first of all an ecological crisis. It is not first of all a crisis concerning our environment. It is first of all a crisis concerning the way we think. We are treating our planet in an inhuman, god-forsaken manner because we see things in an inhuman, god-forsaken way. And we see things in this way because that basically is how we see ourselves.[11]

I believe that Sherrard is right. An adequate response to our predicament demands that we take seriously the link between creation, humankind and God. There cannot be, Sherrard implies, adequate account of one without an integral account

---

[9] Matthew Fox, *The Coming of the Cosmic Christ. The Healing of Mother Earth and the Birth of a Global Renaissance* (San Francisco, 1988), pp. 6–7.

[10] Ibid., p. 1.

[11] *Human Image: World Image. The Death and Resurrection of Sacred Cosmology* (Ipswich, 1992), p. 2.

of the other. Here, I think, is where the contribution of Fr. Dumitru is important. His understanding of creation as the gift of God involves just the sort of integrated vision of God, humankind and the world for which the analysis of our present ecological crisis cries. Yet, as I hope this study will reveal, Fr. Dumitru's purposeful consideration of the meaning of the created order is part of a single thread of theological reflection whose foundations rest firmly within an Orthodox Christian vision of a God who is recognized at once as creator, redeemer and transfigurer.

There are, of course, many standpoints from which one might approach Stăniloae's writings. I do so from the perspective of the Anglican tradition and, more particularly, from within the context of openness and sympathy which has, since 1935 especially, existed between the Church of England and Stăniloae's Romanian Orthodox Church.[12] It may be that Anglicans especially will find Stăniloae a sympathetic voice, an amiable perspective, the representative of one bridge church speaking to another. Overall, this presentation of his theology of creation suggests lines of thought wholly consonant with Anglican theology's strong incarnational thrust. However that may be, though, it is clear to me that the horizons of Stăniloae's thought are sufficiently wide as to speak to the needs and concerns of the wider ecumenical church. Without pursuing them rigorously, therefore, points of contact with the insights of the western tradition feature in this presentation. Chapter 4, 'Christ, Creation and the Cross,' seeks to show this in regard to the theology of the cross, a theological flash-point where

---

[12] In the history of Anglican-Orthodox ecumenism the Romanian Orthodox Church has consistently shown a positive and creative interest. The 'Romanian Thesis' of the Anglican-Orthodox Theological Commission in Bucharest in 1935 – that any discussion of the validity of Anglican Orders must be set within the wider context of Anglican doctrine and sacramental theology – not only resulted in the Romanians' conditional acceptance of Anglican Orders without invoking the principle of economy, but prompted the publication of several important studies on Anglicanism in the Romanian journals *Studii Teologice* and *Ortodoxia*. This rapport was expressed later by the visit of Archbishop Michael Ramsey to Romania in 1965 and by a reciprocal visit by Patriarch Justinian to Britain in the following year.

confessional differences have often been acute. The final chapter brings Stăniloae's rich theology of creation into the sphere of sacramental theology and ecclesiology. There the universal scope of the themes already discussed is earthed in the everyday soil of the worshipping church and in particular the eucharist. A list of published writings in English is provided at the end to enable the interested reader to pursue further study of Stăniloae's theology.

Altogether, I hope that these studies will highlight the quality of freedom in Dumitru Stăniloae's thought. He himself has described that quality of freedom as 'open conciliarity' or 'open catholicity' in which the diversity, the positive contributions, even the limitations of different traditions, are taken into the service of our common quest for sanctification and truth.[13] For that reason alone we Christians in the West, both Orthodox and non-Orthodox, may find Stăniloae's contribution relevant as we seek a comprehensive and unifying vision of faith for the third millennium.

[13] This notion, in Romanian, 'Sobornicitate deschisă,' he expounds in an article in *Ortodoxia*, 23, no. 2 (1971): 165–180.

1

Dumitru Stăniloae (1903–1993): The Man and His World

An appreciation of Dumitru Stăniloae's place within the wider world of modern theology must begin with the religious and cultural contexts that have formed his identity as a person and as a theologian. For despite his desire to articulate a genuinely catholic theology, Stăniloae is keenly aware of the unique vision and sensibility which one's local or national social and cultural context afford. 'Each nation,' he once wrote to a friend, 'possesses its unique gifts.'[1] So, what of the gifts which have shaped Stăniloae's sensibilities as a Romanian Orthodox theologian?

Orthodoxy in Transylvania

Dumitru Stăniloae's native Transylvania, where he was born in 1903, epitomizes the diversity of influences that have shaped Romania's religious culture.[2] As the Roman Province of Dacia it was overrun by Goths and other invaders in the late third

---

[1] A letter from Fr. Stăniloae to A. M. Allchin.

[2] This historical sketch follows that of Eric Tappe, 'The Romanian Church and the West,' *Studies in Church History*, 13 (Oxford, 1976), pp. 277–291, and, where cited, Vlad Georgescu, *The Romanians. A History*, ed. Matei Calinescu, trans. Alexandra Bley-Vroman (Columbus, 1991).

century. Beginning in the eleventh century, Transylvania, the westernmost province of Romania bordering on Hungary, was swept into the current of western European influences when it passed under the hegemony of Catholic Hungary and became barter material between popes and religious orders. As Hungarian expansion became more aggressive in the thirteenth century Saxons and Hungarians began to populate the cities and towns. Amongst the rural population in villages like Fr. Stăniloae's native Vladeni, however, Orthodoxy remained dominant.

In the sixteenth century two other factors complicated the religious life of Romania's people. The first was a wholly non-Christian influence: in 1528 the three Romanian provinces of Transylvania, Wallachia and Moldavia became tribute-paying principalities of the Ottoman Turks. Other new and more enduring influences were the reforming principles that infiltrated from western Europe in the 1530s. Lutheran and Calvinist ideas were strongest among the Saxon and Hungarian inhabitants of Romania's western regions. The Orthodoxy of the indigenous population, however, was accorded the status of a 'tolerated religion' in subordination to the 'received religions' of Catholicism, Lutheranism and Calvinism.

During those years of turbulence and rapidly changing religious demographics the Orthodox population was ruled by non-Orthodox princes of, alternately, Calvinist and Roman Catholic allegiance. The extent to which Orthodox identity was threatened can be seen in one Calvinist prince's request to Cyril Lukaris (1572–1638), the Patriarch of Constantinople, that he assist the prince in the conversion of the Orthodox population to Calvinism![3]

But the Reformation influence brought other, positive, results as well. Surely Romania is the only predominantly Orthodox country whose printed literary history began with the publication of the Romanian Bible and a Lutheran catechism. Both

[3] Cyril Lukaris (1572–1638) is a controversial figure in Orthodox history, not least owing to his sympathy with Calvinist ideas, as his *Confession*, published in Geneva (1629), shows. See Kallistos (Timothy) Ware's discussion in *The Orthodox Church* (Baltimore, 1964), pp. 106–108.

of those works were, in fact, first produced in Stăniloae's native Transylvania where Lutheran influence was strong.

While Protestant currents prevailed in the sixteenth and early seventeenth centuries, a revival of Roman Catholic power began in the middle of the seventeenth century with the coming of the Jesuits. At that time the problems between Orthodox and Catholics of the eastern rite began; they continue to this day.[4] When the metropolitical see of Alba Iulia became Uniate, Transylvania was deprived of an Orthodox metropolitan until 1864 when the city of Sibiu became an Orthodox metropolitanate. Transylvania was, in fact, the scene of persistent missionary efforts on the part of the eastern rite Catholics. Fr. Stăniloae's village knew first-hand the division that such activity often fostered.[5]

The Language Factor

Like Romania's political and religious history, the language also points to the country's intermediate position between Christian East and West. Romanian, unlike the language of any other Orthodox country, stands firmly within the family of western Europe's romance languages. Like French, Italian, Spanish and Portuguese, Romanian evolved out of the *koine* (common) Latin spoken in the Roman province of Dacia. It has preserved its essentially Latin character, yet it has also subsumed Greek and Slavic elements into its vocabulary and, to a lesser extent, into its syntax. The attainment of statehood in 1877 brought an attempt to reintegrate the Romanian language more securely within the western European linguistic tradition. Consequently, there was a conscious desire to re-Romanize the language by means of significant borrowings from French and Italian.

In Fr. Stăniloae's writings we have, then, a significant corpus of indigenous Orthodox theology in a Latin-based language.

---

[4] For a brief history and contemporary assessment of the Uniate situation in Romania, see Janice Broun, 'The Latin-Rite Catholic Church in Romania,' *Religion in Communist Lands*, 12, no. 2 (1984): 168–184.

[5] So comments Ion Bria, 'Vision,' 57. Georgescu maintains that because of ethnic diversity in Transylvania during the first half of this century the potential for ethnic conflict was greatest there (p. 189).

The character of the language, therefore, not only makes for easier access to Romanian Orthodox theological literature by western theologians, but it gives the Romanian Orthodox themselves an ease of access to the western Christian tradition which, for instance, Greeks or Russians do not enjoy in the same way. Here again, Stăniloae's Romanian heritage, his own wide linguistic ability, and the breadth of writings in French, German, Greek, English and Russian which constitute his sources, give comprehensive scope to his theology.

I have underlined such external factors because they are part of the wider context in which we must place and understand Dumitru Stăniloae's theological development and contribution. To know the man and those factors which have shaped his identity is, in large measure, to know his theology. When we encounter Dumitru Stăniloae, therefore, we encounter not simply an Orthodox theologian but a *Romanian* theologian, one who openly acknowledges the way in which cultural, national, regional and even linguistic factors have shaped his theological outlook.

An Orthodox 'Via Media'

The village of Vlădeni where he was born in 1903 was typical of the region: a farming village nestled in a valley, surrounded by forests and mountains. In the province of Transylvania in particular there was a special closeness between the church and the people. Stăniloae described it as 'a sort of ecclesiastical republic,'[6] but one where freedom and care prevailed.

> I was brought up in this spirit [he recalls]: a church that is very important, very near the people, one that occupies itself not only with religious questions but with all of the people's concerns . . . the people possessed the church's whole living tradition.[7]

The time of his first theological study at the Faculty in Cernăuţi was a period when the northern Romanian lands in

---

[6] Marc-Antoine Costa de Beauregard, *Dumitru Staniloae, 'Ose comprendre que Je t'aime'* (Paris, 1983), p. 16. Translations my own.
[7] Ibid., p. 17.

Transylvania were beginning to emerge from the long ascendancy of the Hungarian Calvinist and Catholic presence. Within such a context Stăniloae's early interests focused, predictably perhaps, on the confessional identity of Orthodoxy with a keen sensitivity to the way in which his cultural and regional identity had shaped his outlook.

It is here, I think, that we can begin to see some of the deeper, more subtle factors which have fostered the special rapport felt especially between Anglicans and Romanian Orthodox within the broader domain of Anglican-Orthodox contact. In speaking of the particular ethos of his Romanian Orthodoxy Fr. Dumitru described it as 'eastern latinity,'[8] a phrase that harks back to the very origins of Romania's cultural history as a Roman province. He himself declared:

> We are Latins and, at the same time, Orthodox. There is to be found here an original synthesis between the joyous, open, bright Latin spirit, and the mystical spirituality, the depth of Orthodoxy. We distinguish ourselves from the other Orthodox who are purely eastern, the Greeks and the Russians. There is among us a very Latin rationality, serene, communicative, lively joyous, never superficial or abstract.[9]

This is not to depreciate the Romanian sensitivity to that quality of mystery, which western Christians usually find very compelling in Orthodox religious experience. Far from it. 'It goes deep into God, into mystery,' Stăniloae once affirmed, 'but in the mystery itself there is reason and sense.'[10]

There is also an openness to human expression and an ease in approaching God through simple human sensibilities. He described it this way:

---

[8] Ibid., p. 13. The politico-cultural import of that phrase should not be overlooked. Stăniloae's stress on Romania's Orthodox religious ethos as 'Eastern Latinity' contrasts with the Communist-inspired attempts to rewrite Romanian history so as to magnify the role of the Slavs and to diminish the Roman and Latin aspects. That revisionist agenda began in the 1950s. See Georgescu, p. 241.

[9] Ibid., p. 24.

[10] Ibid.

The Romanian Orthodox interiorizes much of his religious vision, and he lives much of this vision through his intuitive, natural sensibilities, for he doesn't know how to express his religious vision directly. Thus, he will happily – though modestly – express it through ideas; but through art as well, poetry, music, sculpture, painting, and especially in the Art of arts, the liturgy.[11]

In its restraint, its discomfort with extremes, in its modest expressiveness; in its light-heartedness as well as in its reasoned sensitivity to the mystery of God, the religious ethos of Romanian Orthodoxy is pre-eminently one of spiritual balance.[12] Such was Dumitru Stăniloae himself. Those who knew him speak of the sense of proportion in his life-style, and of a keen appreciation for the spiritual dimension in the ordinary, the everyday. Similarly, his theology is marked by proportion. 'His thought', notes one writer, 'is concentrated on the theme of balance; balance in Christ between the absolute transcendence of God and his presence at the very heart of the cosmos.'[13] Here is an approach, a religious sensibility, in tune with the notion of the *via media*, or 'middle way,' understood not as doctrinal compromise but as a fundamental spiritual disposition whose instinctive preference is for the observance of balance and due proportion.

If that disposition toward the living of the Orthodox faith came to Stăniloae as a natural and, in some sense, easy consequence of his native cultural milieu, the particular accents and themes of his thought have emerged out of a long, at times painful, theological journey.

Engaging the Tradition

The Orthodoxy of Stăniloae's youth was still in the grip of Latin categories, language and method as a consequence of the 'western captivity' that began in the seventeenth century.[14] His

---

[11] Ibid., p. 13.
[12] Ibid., p. 23.
[13] Ibid.
[14] See Georges Florovsky, *Ways of Russian Theology (Part One)* (Belmont, 1979), chapters 3 and 5 especially; also see George Maloney, SJ, *A History of Orthodox Theology since 1453* (Belmont, 1976), pp. 271–298.

early theological training, therefore, followed a rationalistic German model based upon the principles of scholastic metaphysics. 'One never had to think about God,' Stăniloae recalled, 'everything had been said.'[15] And so, except for the acquisition of a methodical research technique, he gained little from his initial theological studies, and even abandoned his interest in dogmatics.

When he turned to the study of church history he was equally frustrated. Although in the course of study he discovered the Hesychast tradition of spirituality and theology, his scholastic manuals described it as 'strange.'[16] At this early stage he became acutely aware of the plight of his own Orthodox theological tradition. While, on the one hand, the great exponent of Hesychasm, Gregory Palamas (c. 1296–1359), was revered as one of the greatest Orthodox saints, on the other hand, the tradition which Palamas represented was virtually unknown. Instead of finding a theology rooted in a personal encounter with God in prayer, he found a cerebral, academic theology divorced both from personal faith and the life of the church. Despite this, he never lost interest in Palamas and Hesychasm. His later study, *The Life and Teaching of Gregory Palamas* (1938), constitutes one of the earliest attempts to revive the theological insights of Gregory Palamas within the Orthodox tradition, and that influence continued as a fundamental component of Stăniloae's perspective.[17]

Still unhappy with his theological curriculum, he left the theological faculty and moved to Bucharest to study literature. It was a period of questioning, discouragement and doubt. But at that point, when Stăniloae's interest in the study of theology hung in the balance, the influence of Metropolitan Balan of

---

[15] Beauregard, p. 18. This biographical sketch follows Beauregard.

[16] Ibid., p. 19. As a spiritual tradition associated especially with Mt. Athos, Hesychasm emphasizes inner stillness through the practice of the prayer of the heart. Its theological implications extend to a distinction between the *essence* and the uncreated *energies* of God. On Hesychasm generally, see Ware, *Orthodox Church*, pp. 72–80.

[17] The standard treatments in English are John Meyendorff's two works, *A Study of Gregory Palamas* (London, 1964), and *St. Gregory Palamas and Orthodox Spirituality* (Crestwood, 1974).

Sibiu was decisive. He took a special personal interest in Stăniloae and through his persuasion Stăniloae returned to his study of theology with a new enthusiasm. Not only did he learn Russian in order to read the new theology of men like Sergei Bulgakov, writing in Paris, but he also exposed himself to the wider intellectual milieu of the western tradition in thinkers such as Kant, Hegel and Schopenauer.

With sustained interest Metropolitan Balan awarded him a grant for study in Athens. Stăniloae himself had requested it; he hoped to learn Greek and study the fathers. But there, as at home, he found the patristic tradition largely ignored. Instead, therefore, he began research on the seventeenth-century patriarch Dositheos of Jerusalem (1641–1707) and his relations with Romania. This issued in a doctoral thesis entitled *The Life and Activity of Patriarch Dositheos of Jerusalem* (1928).

Still under the aegis of the metropolitan of Sibiu, Stăniloae was sent to Munich between 1928 and 1929 to study Byzantine history. Like many others at the time, the young Romanian was excited by the ferment caused by Karl Barth's 'Commentary on Romans', the second edition of which appeared in 1922. In contrast to the stultifying academic theology of previous years, the new 'dialectical theology' was a theology in which God was not just a theological premise, but a Person who comes to man in judgment and who challenges man's existence. This dialectical theology acknowledged that all formulas and propositions about God must mislead in the very act of being received by us. 'I gained from this theology,' Stăniloae later acknowledged, 'the affirmation of a living God, the affirmation of the transcendence of God before man.'[18] There were aspects to be criticized as well, however. His simultaneous study of Gregory Palamas's theology, with its distinction between 'essence' and 'energy' – the unknowable and the knowable in God, respectively – provided Stăniloae with a qualification to Barth's over-emphasis upon divine transcendence by allowing for a way of speaking about God's real involvement with humankind and the world without compromising his essential unknowability.

[18] Beauregard, p. 22.

His lifetime's work as a teacher began in 1929 when, at the behest of Metropolitan Balan, he took up a lectureship in dogmatic theology at the Theological Institute in Sibiu, the provincial capital of Transylvania. This period, extending until 1946, was one of significant theological creativity. His early years as a teacher witnessed not only Stăniloae's marriage to his wife Maria, and ordination to the priesthood, but a growing involvement in pragmatic pastoral issues. At the national level it expressed itself through his role as editor of the newspaper *Telegraf Roman* which advocated an Orthodox viewpoint in issues of national life and culture. An involvement in and sensitivity toward the common life and opinions of his fellow Romanians was an ever-present aspect of his theological reflection. He was, as A. M. Allchin notes, a man who never lost touch with the faith and experience of a great variety of people in all walks of life.[19] Even his highly sophisticated assimilations of patristic or Byzantine theology and contemporary thought were informed by this rootedness in the common, shared experience of the faith. Again as Allchin observes, the question 'how would the villagers at home feel about this?' was part of his approach even to difficult theological problems.[20] The pastoral orientation of his editorial work confirmed that orientation.

The period between the world wars when Stăniloae's involvement in church life was growing was one of passionate and profound confrontation of ideas in Romania. Amid the polarities of traditionalism and modernism, nationalism and internationalism, orthodoxy and 'western materialism', we find Stăniloae deepening his appreciation for the Romanian Orthodox cultural and theological tradition. A lasting influence was exercised upon Stăniloae by the militantly Orthodox journalist and poet Nichifor Crainic (1898–1972), who championed attempts to define a specifically Romanian mentality and return natural culture to traditional Christian roots.[21] In

---

[19] Introduction to D. Stăniloae, *Holiness*, p. v.
[20] Ibid.
[21] Georgescu, p. 205. Stăniloae collaborated with Crainic in the publication of the eminent review *Gândirea (Thought)*; it was published between the years 1921–1944. *Gândirea* was but one sign of the efflorescence of art and literature

fact it was chiefly Crainic's influence in enlarging the circle of theological concerns that encouraged Stăniloae's interest in mystical theology and the spiritual implications of dogma.[22]

Stăniloae was well-placed, therefore, to address issues of theology which were not only religious in the strict sense. At the level of his country's cultural life Stăniloae wrote on behalf of an Orthodox culture over against the more secular Romanian intelligentsia. The philosopher-poet Lucian Blaga (1895–1961) was a pre-eminent example of those who, while sharing the desire to identify a distinct Romanian spirit, sought to do so apart from the Orthodox religious inheritance. Stăniloae's public controversy with Blaga won for him a national reputation.

Theological Conversion

During these years at Sibiu a decisive shift occurred in Stăniloae's theological perspective. Soon after his arrival he published a translation of the Greek dogmatician Chrestos Androutsos's *Handbook of Dogmatics* (1930) which represented the 'old school' with which his theological training had begun.[23] As he translated this work he became more and more dissatisfied with it. The publications which followed, therefore, reveal a profound reorientation toward a wholly different theological method and vision. Mention has already been made

---

following the First World War and the incorporation of Transylvania into greater Romania. On Crainic's contribution to Romania's national and religious life, see the unpublished thesis of Christine M. Hall, ' "Jesus in my Country." The Theology of Nichiphor Crainic with special reference to the cultural and historical background' (University of London, King's College, 1986).

[22] So Stăniloae described Crainic's influence in Romanian theology in his commendation of Crainic's *Sfînţenia-împlinirea Umanului* in 1993. *Sfînţenia* was originally given as a course of lectures in the Faculty of Theology in Bucharest in 1935–1936.

[23] Of this work, published in 1907, and others like it produced in Greece during this period, Kallistos Ware notes that 'it is a theology of the University lecture room, but not a *mystical* theology, as in the days of Byzantium when theological scholarship flourished in the monastic cell as well as in the university' (*Orthodox Church*, p. 148).

of his pioneering study of the theology of Gregory Palamas
published in 1938. A more emphatic and influential statement
of Stăniloae's own theological renewal came five years later
when in 1943, while still at Sibiu, he published *Jesus Christ, or
the Restoration of Man*. Not only is the influence of the thought
of the seventh-century Byzantine theologian Maximus the
Confessor (*c*.580–662) pervasive in this work, but in it emerge
several themes which will characterize his theology as a
whole.[24] In particular, he reclaimed Maximus' theology of the
creative *Logos* and of cosmic transfiguration. But even more
importantly, he developed his own theology of *hypostasis* and
an understanding of man as eternal person.[25] In the *Orthodox
Dogmatic Theology* we see the maturation of his theology of
person as a fundamental component of his meditation on the
meaning of Christian dogmas. Those years at Sibiu signified Fr. Stăniloae's final rejection of scholastic categories of
thought. Henceforth, all his writings would be characterized
by a dynamic, existential orientation, and by the desire, as
Stăniloae himself put it, 'to tie together the meaning of the
dogmas of the Church with the interior life of man.'[26] It is pre-
eminently patristic theology, in keeping with Fr. Georges
Florovsky's description of such theology as being rooted in
'the decisive commitment of faith,' a theology with spiritual
consequences.[27]

During those same years, in fact, Stăniloae was preparing a
Romanian edition of the great anthology of Orthodox spiritual
writings, the *Philokalia*, which was first published in Venice in
1782. Stăniloae was following a rich Romanian tradition of

[24] The influence of the theologian Nichifor Crainic on the thought of
Stăniloae is an area for investigation. Crainic's course of lectures on mystical
theology, published as *Holiness: the Fulfilment of Humankind* in 1935–1936 re-
introduced the theology of St. Maximus. In 1978, the same year his *Orthodox
Dogmatic Theology* was published, Stăniloae's *Commentaries on St. Maximus the
Confessor* appeared in a Greek edition edited by P. Nellas and published by
the Apostaliki Diakonia Publishing House (Athens).

[25] Bria, 'Vision,' 54.

[26] Beauregard, p. 28.

[27] 'Patristic Theology and the Ethos of the Orthodox Church,' in *Aspects of
Church History* (Belmont, 1975), p. 17.

interest in the hesychastic spirituality of the *Philokalia*. In 1763 Paissy Valichkovsky became abbot of the monastery of Neamţ in Moldavia and produced in 1793 a Slavonic translation of the *Philokalia*. The first three volumes of Stăniloae's Romanian translation appeared in 1947. More than a translation, this work is a fully annotated edition constituting one of the major literary achievements of modern Romanian religious culture. The twelfth and final volume appeared in 1982.

The period following the Second World War brought many changes to Romanian life. Politically, the decisive shift from authoritarianism to Stalin's totalitarianism took place.[28] The establishment of a Marxist state as a result of Soviet occupation during the war affected church life profoundly and, at times, violently. It is surprising to find, however, that the life of the church and state remained in many ways intertwined. Justinian, who became Patriarch in 1948,[29] was at first violently criticized in the West for his accommodation with the communist régime. In fact, the compromises which he made with the state enabled him to achieve some remarkable reforms within the church. But the situation was, in fact, highly oppressive for the church. Romanian Orthodoxy has, nevertheless, displayed a spiritual and theological vigour unparalleled in any of the former eastern-bloc Orthodox churches.[30]

The same year, 1948, which ushered in widespread nationalization throughout the country, saw major legal revisions giving each ecclesial entity in Romania responsibility for its own theological education.[31] Two years before, Fr. Stăniloae had moved to Bucharest to teach dogmatics at the newly formed Theological Institute. As a professor at the Institute he fought vigorously to convince his church's hierarchy of the need for a freer approach to the study and writing of theology, one rooted

[28] See Georgescu, pp. 222–232.
[29] The Romanian church was granted autocephaly in 1925.
[30] Ware, *Orthodox Church*, pp. 175–176.
[31] Mirca Păcurariu, 'Istoria învăţămîntului teologic în Biserica Ortodoxă Română,' *Biserica Ortodoxă Română*, nos. 9–10 (1981): 979–1017: see also A. Johansen, *Theological Study in the Romanian Orthodox Church Under Communist Rule* (London, 1961): and *De La Théologie Orthodoxe Roumaine Des Origins à Nos Jours* (Bucharest, 1974), *passim*.

in the life of the church and emerging out of the personal commitment of faith.[32] As a teacher Stăniloae could be deceptively simple. As one student put it: 'unlike other teachers who seemed to want to make the notion of God complicated, Fr. Stăniloae insisted that the notion of God was really very simple.'[33] For some students he was too simple; they felt he did not live up to his reputation. For many others, though, Stăniloae's desire to stress the essential simplicity of the notion of God brought an unexpected freedom to their study of theology. It was the outworking at the level of the intellect of the simplicity and centeredness of the *Philokalia's* spiritual teaching. Other fruitful concerns arose in response to the questions posed by wider ecumenical contact and dialogue. Writings on interconfessional problems have been a constant feature of his theological reflection as his contributions to the Romanian theological journal *Ortodoxia*, for example, make plain.

Although the general literary culture of Stalinist Romania was sterile in the post-war years, it was a productive period for Stăniloae's own theological writing. Indeed, even as a married priest with a family he became a key figure in the remarkable revival of the religious life during those years, and he became a well-known and much revered figure among Romania's vibrant monastic communities. In 1948 several more volumes of the Romanian *Philokalia* appeared. Then in 1952 he published a volume entitled *Orthodox Christian Doctrine*, followed six years later by a *Manual of Dogmatic and Symbolic Theology* in two volumes which he co-authored with another Romanian theologian, Nicolae Chitescu. Owing to publications such as these, writers now refer to this period as a rebirth of Romanian dogmatic theology. In this rediscovery of theology's 'authentic patristic spirit' Stăniloae occupied a key position.[34]

[32] Clément, p. 12. Officially Stăniloae was Professor of Ascetical and Mystical Theology.

[33] So remarked Fr. Ioan Popescu, a student of Fr. Stăniloae's in the 1970s, in an interview with the author (June, 1993).

[34] Ion Bria, 'A Look at Contemporary Romanian Orthodox Theology,' *Sobornost*, 6:5 (1972): 330.

Witness and Imprisonment

While the theological creativity and spiritual renewal in post-war Romania are to be noted, so too must the arbitrary victimization of the population by the Communist régime. Although, following the war, Orthodox clergy had become one of the largest groups of political prisoners, the momentum of repression had not been consistent. But in response to uprisings in Poland and Hungary in the mid-1950s the government clamped down again.[35] Between 1958 and 1962 a gap appears in Fr. Stăniloae's biography. He was incarcerated at Aiud Prison together with other churchmen and intellectuals. Stăniloae himself was never physically abused, but he knew of the various abuses which other prisoners suffered. The hardships were ameliorated only by the camaraderie between the prisoners. Some of them were extraordinary indeed. In the early 1960s, for instance, Stăniloae came into contact with the brilliant economist, philosopher and mystic Petre Ţuţea (1902–1991).[36] But whereas for Ţuţea the prison was a place for open, indeed heroic Christian *apologia* in the face of physical and mental brutality, Stăniloae's witness was less overt, in some sense more interior. He acknowledged later that during his time in prison he first was able to practice the perpetual invocation of the Name of Jesus.[37] The Hesychast tradition was not merely a scholarly interest but a lifegiving inner reality. Of those years of imprisonment he said little. His silence was the most eloquent testimony to the degree of his own suffering and that of family and friends. He admitted, though, that the years of imprisonment taught him that theology was not sufficiently 'in touch' with the people. Here was yet another incentive toward the existential approach to dogma that he championed.[38]

[35] Georgescu, p. 237.
[36] See Alexandru Popescu's article 'Petre Ţuţea (1902–1991): the Urban Hermit of Romanian Spirituality,' *Religion, State and Society*, 23, no. 4 (1995): 319–341.
[37] 'Préface' to Stăniloae, *Prière*, p. 11.
[38] Bria, 'Dogmatic Theology', 332.

The Orthodox Dogmatic Theology

He returned to his teaching at the Institute in Bucharest in 1963 and continued there for another ten years before his retirement in 1973. Five years later, in 1978, the fruit of almost sixty years of writing on theology and spirituality issued in the publication of his three-volume *Orthodox Dogmatic Theology* or, as it is in its first volume in English, *The Experience of God*. As the only modern comprehensive treatment of dog-matic theology, Stăniloae's work fills a noticeable gap in contemporary Orthodox literature. But even a cursory reading of his *Dogmatic Theology* reveals a perspective deserving much wider reception. This is partly due to the ecumenical scope of his concerns. Most readers will find insights from their own tradition co-opted into Stăniloae's masterly synthesis. In that sense, Stăniloae's *Dogmatic Theology* is unlike most other expositions of Orthodox theology. His approach, it has been noted, differs from those who present Orthodoxy in the form of a theological introduction for non-Orthodox readers.[39] Instead, we find a theological perspective shaped by the demands and challenges commonly experienced by Christians living in the last quarter of the twentieth century. If his *Dogmatic Theology* has any claim to be received and pondered by Christians of every tradition, it is because the theology it expounds has emerged out of a life-long endeavour to respond to those urgent challenges posed to all Christians, indeed to all men and women living in modern industrialized society. For this reason Fr. Stăniloae himself described it as a 'secular' theology, that is, one which gives whole-hearted attention to the value of the world, and which attempts to facilitate humankind's 'true development' toward genuine *humanitas*.[40]

An equally compelling characteristic of the *Orthodox Dogmatic Theology* is its overall style. It is notable for attempting to by-pass out-dated theological structures and language in an effort to secure for Orthodox theology a more universal hearing.

---

[39] Bria, 'Vision,' 54.
[40] *DT*, I, p. 105.

Moreover the work has, as Ion Bria observes, a personal, confessing style, a quality not often found in Orthodox theological literature.[41] In this we may discern how, at least for Fr. Stăniloae, the dogmas and doctrines of the Christian faith are not objective formulas demanding intellectual affirmation alone. They are truths whose purpose is to lead us to Christ, truths by which we live, in which we have a stake.

In the years immediately prior to and following his retirement from active teaching Stăniloae had occasion to travel in the West. The visits involved contact with his fellow-Orthodox, of course, but with western friends as well. In 1968–1969 he made the first of several trips to England. His time among the Anglican Sisters of the Love of God in Oxford provided the occasion for one of his earliest publications in English, *The Victory of the Cross*. Subsequent visits confirmed those links and gave ample testimony to Stăniloae's open style of Orthodoxy. As A. M. Allchin remarks in reflection upon those visits:

> It was typical for him too that it was a Western Cathedral which evoked his amazement. Though he could be severely critical of aspects of Western theology, he was always ready to learn and receive from the traditions of Western Christianity. He had no doubt of the centrality of Orthodoxy in the Christian world and he sought constantly to articulate the fullness and balance of the Orthodox vision of the faith. But for him that vision was always an open and inclusive thing, never something closed or exclusive.[42]

In retirement with his wife Maria in their cramped apartment in Bucharest Fr. Stăniloae continued to write and speak. He was a frequent contributor to symposia sponsored by the World Council of Churches and the Faith and Order Commission.

After the Revolution of 1989 Romania's doors opened considerably. A marked feature of the new period was an explosion in publishing. A number of his own works, including his early foundational studies, were reissued, as were those of his deceased contemporaries. It was Stăniloae's privilege to

---

[41] Bria, 'Vision,' 58.
[42] 'Dumitru Stăniloae,' *Sobornost/ECR*, 16:1 (1994): 43.

commend to a new generation the notable achievements of an earlier era whose voices had been unjustly silenced.

Even in retirement and old age Stăniloae enjoyed his wide contacts; they were personal expressions of the openness which the reality of God engenders. In a Christmas letter to an Anglican friend Stăniloae concluded in halting English, 'The reality seen in God is so deep and rich that we arrive never at end.'[43] That openness, that innate ecumenicity, gives to Dumitru Stăniloae's theology an unusual importance in our common quest for a more universal expression of Christian faith. Such a characteristic was for Stăniloae not simply a concession in an ecumenical age but a response demanded by the very nature of the Gospel.

> Every situation is a call from God who asks us to take a stand. Each man whom we encounter is a word from God. Other people are speakers, images of the Word of God, in the image of God's hypostatic Word. They are images who speak; who speak to us as the very Word of God speaks to us, as Christ speaks. God has given others to us to call us, and to them we must respond.[44]

Such is the motivation and goal of all that Dumitru Stăniloae taught and wrote. If through his writings we are enabled to appropriate that disposition even a little more deeply, his gift to us will have been enormous.

---

[43] Letter to A. M. Allchin.
[44] Beauregard, p. 29.

2

Creation and the Experience of God

The theme of creation with which this study is largely concerned pervades Stăniloae's mature writings. This is as true of his ascetical and devotional writings as it is of his dogmatic or systematic works. English-speaking readers will naturally gravitate toward his systematic work, the *Orthodox Dogmatic Theology*.[1] Indeed, there is much there which concerns our theme. In pursuing Stăniloae's discussion of creation, however, his *Orthodox Dogmatic Theology* can only serve as a kind of distillation of the interrelated web of concerns and insights which make up his theology of creation. Therefore, although in this chapter we deal with the *Dogmatic Theology*, subsequent chapters will develop Stăniloae's understanding with reference to a broader range of his writings, some in English, others in Romanian, some theological, others devotional. In this way the prismatic quality of Stăniloae's consideration of the creation theme can be appreciated since the different genres in which he treats it refract his insights with distinct but complementary hues.

---

[1] Despite the fact that the quotations here can be found in *The Experience of God*, I have used my own translations from the Romanian edition of the *Dogmatic Theology* since they pre-date the appearance of the English edition.

Having said that it would be wrong to think that the creation theme is somehow tangential to Stăniloae's theological vision, a mere embellishment which happens to strike a contemporary chord. While a modern reader may indeed find that it strikes a chord, he or she cannot help but be struck by the thoroughly integrated place which the topic occupies in Stăniloae's theology. It is not an afterthought but part of a seamless fabric of Christian experience and theological reflection gradually woven over a lifetime. The previous chapter, with its allusions to Stăniloae's deeply rural sensibilities, indicates the attitude that forms the backdrop to this particular theological concern. To know the man is in large measure to know his theology. So how does Stăniloae develop that inner sensibility into an explicit theology?

The answer to that question, which the following chapters will explore, cannot better begin than where Stăniloae himself does: with the two opening chapters of the *Orthodox Dogmatic Theology* entitled 'Natural Revelation' and 'Supernatural Revelation.' My hope is, first, that the discussion of salient features of Stăniloae's exposition will fix the groundwork for aspects of his theology of creation discussed in subsequent chapters; and second, that the reader will appreciate something of the overall character of Stăniloae's theological approach through a consideration of this particular theme.

A Style of Personal Confession

The opening chapter of the *Orthodox Dogmatic Theology* may puzzle readers. Those expecting a style of presentation in which topics are precisely distinguished, where self-critical prolegomena abound, will be disappointed. Stăniloae provides no such pedagogical help, no explicit points of reference. Instead, the reader enters into the subject directly and without any pause for the author to explain what he seeks to do or how he will proceed. The reader may therefore feel at sea, as if he or she has suddenly entered into an ongoing conversation whose origin and direction are not apparent. Yet upon inspection it is clear that a subtle and comprehensive rationale guides Stăniloae's disarming narrative style. In explaining such a direct entry into the subject of dogmatics Karl Barth once remarked that it might well indicate a 'very conscious, well-thought-out, scientific' attitude.[2] I think this can be said of Stăniloae. The *Dogmatic Theology* does not seek to burden the reader with the weighty theological investigation which lies behind it. Instead it presents those findings in a distilled, unencumbered way, in a style of writing which, as others have noted, has a refreshing air of personal confession.[3]

The two opening chapters of the *Orthodox Dogmatic Theology* introduce three foundational elements in Stăniloae's understanding of theology. The first, creation as revelation, is obviously relevant to the concern of this study; the second, similarly, has a direct bearing which another chapter will develop in more detail, namely, the relationship between humankind and the cosmos; the third concerns the relation between nature and grace (to use a convenient western phrase). Clearly, though, the first topic is most important as a foundation for what will follow.

Creation as Revelation

In Dumitru Stăniloae's theology of the created order we encounter one of the most interesting and challenging aspects of his theological vision. It has been noted that, in contrast to other Latin-based languages in which the word for 'world' is derived from *mundus* (e.g. Fr. *monde*, Ital. *mondo*), the Romanian word, *lume*, is taken from the Latin *lumen*, 'light'.[4] It suggests that the world is a theophany, transparent to the light of God. That linguistic feature goes far to explain, I think, why Stăniloae does not take up the subject of creation at a later stage in his exposition, as in the case of many if not most systematic theologies. Rather, he treats it at the very beginning as one of the first principles out of which the possibility of theology – reflection on the experience of God – arises. Creation, he wishes

---

[2] Karl Barth, *Church Dogmatics*, 5 vols., trans. G. T. Thomson (New York, 1936), I, 1, p. 26.

[3] So Ion Bria, 'Vision,' 58.

[4] Clément, in his '*Préface*' to the French translation of the *Orthodox Dogmatic Theology*, *Le génie de l'Orthodoxie*, p. 13.

to affirm, is not a neutral factor for theology, but the fact and condition which allows us to experience and speak of God at all. Indeed, despite the seeming division between the subject matter of the first two chapters of the *Dogmatic Theology*, 'natural revelation' and 'supernatural revelation' respectively, the burden of Stăniloae's exposition is to stress their integrated character.

Stăniloae once remarked: 'We have made the distinction between heaven and earth far too absolute and far too neat. There is constant overlap.'[5] It is noteworthy that Stăniloae puts that view formally in the opening paragraph of the *Dogmatic Theology*. Its entire exposition of the Christian vision begins with an assertion of the significance of creation in God's act of revealing himself and his will for humankind.

> The Orthodox Church does not separate natural revelation and supernatural. Natural revelation is known and fully understood in light of the supernatural revelation: and natural revelation is given and maintained by God's continual action upon nature.[6]

In this programmatic statement, largely inspired by the vision of St. Maximus the Confessor, as so much of his thought is, Stăniloae challenges the autonomous character of 'natural revelation', such as western theology has commonly viewed it. Indeed, the whole notion of an autonomous creation disconnected from divine energy and explicable apart from the divine agenda is quietly yet firmly set aside. In Stăniloae's hands the Maximian perspective enables him to expand the sphere of explicit divine influence into those areas which might be viewed as outside or beneath the 'supernatural.' In fact, although he uses the terminology, there is much in Stăniloae's treatment which begs the question whether it is useful to talk of the 'natural' and 'supernatural' at all. The created world of Maximus which Stăniloae adopts as his own starting-point, is a world which is, to use

---

[5] Allchin, 'Stăniloae,' 42.
[6] *DT*, I, p. 9.

C. S. Lewis's apt phrase, 'drenched in deity.'[7] The revelatory capacity and potential of the world is for Stăniloae based on a belief that there is a fundamental continuity of purpose between nature and supernature, the created and the revealed. If the two are to be distinguished, then such a distinction pertains not so much to the content of what they reveal as to the circumstance, the power, and the directness of their revelatory roles.

In the passage of the *Ambigua* which inspires that view Maximus argues that the content of the natural law (*ho phýsikos nómos*) and of the supernatural and revealed law written in the Bible (*ho gráptos nómos*) are *in substance the same*. When the natural law is understood spiritually, the two laws speak with one voice.[8]

For his part, though, Stăniloae wishes to qualify Maximus's assertion. 'This affirmation,' he explains, 'should perhaps be taken more in this sense, that the two revelations are not divorced from one another.' For Stăniloae this means that revelation *through the created order*, which is for Stăniloae the real import of the phrase 'natural revelation,' is the 'framework' within which supernatural revelation takes place. The image of a frame, like that of a lens, is a serious theological simile. Creation acts as the circumscribed glass through which the divine light may shine. So, this framework, constituted by the created order, is more than an arena within which the supernatural revelation occurs autonomously. Supernatural revelation or revelation through a direct divine act, word, or image (that is the import of the phrase 'supernatural revelation' for Stăniloae) does not supplant the natural order or act wholly apart from it. Rather, the supernatural action is, as it were, addressed to and through the natural context; supernature addresses nature and supports the 'inner movement' with which God has from the first blessed his creation. Supernatural revelation is not, therefore, simply revelatory in itself. In using

[7] C. S. Lewis, *English Literature in the Sixteenth Century Excluding Drama* (Oxford, 1954), p. 457.

[8] *Ambigua, Patrologia Graeca*, 91:1149C–1152B (henceforth cited as *PG*, with volume and column).

the created order it actualizes creation's revelatory potential. Stăniloae puts it this way: 'Supernatural revelation places natural revelation itself in a clearer light.'[9]

This congruity between the created and the supernatural orders is basic to Stăniloae's theological vision and is part of the implicit rationale which he brings to this theological exposition. The attentive reader will see it operate in the discussion of particular themes in subsequent chapters. While it has an application to Stăniloae's theological 'method' as a whole, this parallelism, if we can call it that, plays a key part in his exposition of themes particular to the first volume of the *Orthodox Dogmatic Theology*, namely, the attributes of God and the doctrine of the Trinity. However, the argument which Stăniloae develops as an introduction to those doctrinal themes is also relevant to the theme of creation.

Rationality and Personhood, Human and Divine

Stăniloae asserts that the content, or medium, of revelation through the created order is, simply, the cosmos and humankind. The important feature of that assertion is the link between the cosmos and humankind. We profitably follow Stăniloae's line of thinking when, having asserted the lens quality of the creation, he moves on to identify the place of humankind and the natural order within creation as a whole. His overall purpose is to set up his discussion of the Christian doctrine of the Trinity taken up later in volume one by establishing the notion of 'Personal divine reality' as a 'natural dogma.' It is an attempt to use the relationship between man and the cosmos, human experience and the world, as a lens through which the trinitarian reality of God can shine.

Many of the assumptions which Stăniloae brings to this dense argument are influenced by Maximus the Confessor. Such, for instance, is his emphasis on the solidarity between humankind and creation. Maximus's twin view of humankind as a 'little world' (*microcosmos*) and of the cosmos as an 'enlarged humanity' (*macanthropos*) underpins Stăniloae's

---

[9] *DT*, I, p. 9.

whole approach. Lars Thunberg explains the relevance of this Maximian view which we find in Stăniloae's theology:

> Man is, first of all, presented here as a being in all respects *in the middle* between the extremes of creation, to which he has a natural relationship. He was brought into being as an all-containing workshop, binding all together in himself. As such he has been given the power of unification, thanks to his proper relationship to his own different parts. Man was further brought into being as the last of God's creatures, because he was to be a natural *link* (*sýndesmos*) between all creation, mediating (*mesiteuōn*) between the extremes through the elements of his own nature. Man was thus called to bring into one unity in relation to God as Cause that which was naturally distinguished, starting with his own division . . . And from there he is in a position to go on and unite the world in itself and bring it into an harmonious relationship with God.[10]

These are themes which will reappear throughout subsequent chapters. Thunberg's description of Maximus's anthropology is relevant here because it points to the basis of the intelligibility of the world to humankind as Stăniloae understands it. Most important in humankind's experience in the world is the knowability of the cosmos, its capacity to bear meaning for and through human persons. Humankind's rational power to discern a rationality within the world, to see it as *cosmos* rather than *chaos*, attests, Stăniloae argues, to conscious Reason as the power and source behind, above and below the created order.

But Stăniloae wants to take the evidential force of rationality in man's experience of the world further. For Stăniloae, our experience in and with creation points beyond to a transcendent reality, namely God. Stăniloae sees in Maximus's notion of the fulfillment of the rationality, including the end or purpose, of

---

[10] *Microcosm and Mediator. The Theological Anthropology of Maximus the Confessor* (Lund, 1965), p. 148. A more concise treatment of Maximus's thought is in Thunberg's *Man and the Cosmos. The Vision of St. Maximus the Confessor* (Crestwood, 1985). Just below the surface of Stăniloae's discussion in Chapter One of the *DT* lies Maximus's important doctrine of the *Logos* and the *logoi* of creation; on that, see Chapter 4 below.

the creation in the rational human person, a paradigm for understanding humankind in its transcendent vocation God-ward. The essence of the argument goes like this: just as the rationality or meaning of the sub-personal creation is fulfilled in the creation's relationship with the rational human person, so the human person is fulfilled in its relationship with the infinite or eternal Person, God. In a key passage where the parallel of personal intelligibility is explored Stăniloae explains himself like this:

> If the rationality of the lower, impersonal order finds fulfillment and meaning in service of human being, which is higher than mere nature, then that higher nature of a free and conscious person aspires to find for itself the fulfillment of its rationality and its desire for meaning . . . in communion with a transcendent and free person.[11]

The personal character of this transcendent and free person follows, Stăniloae argues, from the actuality of our own person-hood understood in terms of two defining characteristics, self-consciousness and freedom. Together they form the basis of the distinctive human capacity: communion. Moreover, Stăniloae goes on,

> if the higher relationship between persons is realized in com-munion, our full and eternally satisfying relationship must consist in a communion with a being which is personal in character and endowed with infinity and freedom.[12]

Again, the paradigmatic quality of our relationship with the created order, the evidential force of our own personal existence, is stressed:

> Just as the human being, as the most exalted being in the world, is a person and, as such, is aware of the meaning of the whole lower order of nature which in him is somehow fulfilled, even so the human being must find the fulfillment of its meaning, together with the meanings of all the gradations of nature beneath it, in a person who is aware of that meaning and of the meanings of the

[11] *DT*, I, p. 17.
[12] Ibid.

sub-personal world. Only a still higher person, and in the final analysis only supreme Person, can be aware of the meaning of existence as a whole, as humankind is aware of existence beneath it . . . Our being cannot find fulfillment as personal being except in communion with a higher personal being . . .'[13]

But Stăniloae is emphatic that this higher, supreme personal being is also eternal. It must be, since the meaning and value which our rationality ascribes to our created existence, the world, and one another, would be irrational if they merely ended in death. Therefore, he says,

> only the eternity of a personal communion with a source of *absolute life* offers to all human persons the fulfillment of meaning. At the same time, that source also accords the possibility of an eternal and perfect communion among human persons themselves.[14]

At this point the reader may think that Stăniloae's concern is decidedly anthropocentric. Therefore, precisely at this point he reintroduces the world. Its rationality, its meaning, is completed by the rationality of a person, and chiefly by the supreme Person whose very existence seeks to foster personal communion. That supreme Person, then, has created the world as a means for interpersonal dialogue between the divine Person and human persons. Thus creation, its uses and meanings, are ultimately linked with the in-built aspirations of human persons. The world, Stăniloae continues, is a means of 'dialogue' – a word with a rich meaning in Stăniloae's vocabulary, as a later chapter will show – in fulfillment of those aspirations between the supreme rational Person, God, and rational human persons.[15] The rationality of the created order is fulfilled by the active, free engagement of rational human persons who find their meaning fulfilled in active communion with other human persons and with the supreme Person, God.[16]

---

[13] Ibid., p. 18.
[14] Ibid., p. 19; italics mine.
[15] Ibid., p. 20.
[16] Ibid., pp. 21–22.

'A Natural Dogma'

What Stăniloae has thus far described he sees as the content of faith asserted by the meaning of existence. Such a faith, he says, 'compels' recognition 'on the bases of the evidence in nature.'[17] In a striking phrase Stăniloae describes the core of insights discussed so far as 'so to speak natural dogmas.'[18] With its implied continuity between the realms of nature and grace and a sense of the revelational potential of the created order it succinctly expresses the Maximian colour in Stăniloae's vision of the world. It is not that such natural dogma signifies 'notices' or 'preambles' of saving faith, as in classical western Catholic thought, that is, preparatory insights whose content must then be substantially complemented by the saving truths known only by revelation. In Stăniloae's scheme any substantive difference distinguishing natural from revealed dogma has partly to do with the clarity and partly to do with the faculty by which we perceive them. In keeping with Stăniloae's judgment that these two sources of God's address to us are not divorced from one another, natural revelation and supernatural revelation, as distinct categories, represent two degrees of perception. How are they related? How do they differ? What determines the different degrees of perception?

As we have seen, Stăniloae attributes a great deal of evidential force to human existence and experience. His analysis of humankind's existential condition allows for the assertion of the existence of supreme, eternal Person who is described in terms of interpersonal communion both within itself and with human persons. Although the evidential force for this 'natural dogma' – the trinitarian mystery and humankind's participation in it – exists on the basis of the evidence in nature, that very natural evidence is called into question by death, the universal experience of mortality. So, while human experience, precisely as *personal* experience, points to a supreme personal reality in whom it is fulfilled in communion, the inescapable fact of death contradicts that evidence. In the face

[17] Ibid., p. 21.
[18] Ibid.

of death we are forced to ask: how can our fulfillment in eternal communion with a supreme Person be possible? The hopeful evidence of reason is in the end contradicted by the irrational fact of death.

The Resurrection: Recreating of the Evidential Force of Human Experience

That line of reasoning brings Stăniloae to the second chapter of the *Dogmatic Theology*. Here the power of supernatural faith is added to the testimony of 'natural faith' by way of 'confirmation' and 'completion.' Because death is the flashpoint which weakens the evidential force of natural revelation, the confirmatory power of supernatural revelation is focused in the resurrection. The power unleashed by Christ's resurrection is a power of faith which complements mere natural knowledge and natural faith. Whereas purely rational knowledge and even natural faith are subject to doubt as to our human destiny in the face of death, the 'knowledge' that is engendered by faith in the resurrection is not so limited. On the basis of faith in Christ's resurrection the evidential force of human experience is freed from the constraints of death and so from the element of doubt generated by the fact of death. 'Therefore,' Stăniloae explains,

> supernatural Revelation confirms the evidence of those points of natural faith wherein a higher, eternal meaning of existence flickers. Supernatural Revelation strengthens that natural evidence in so far as it completes it, both through the knowledge which such supernatural Revelation brings to humankind, namely, that through sin and death it has been brought to an unnatural condition, and through the help which it gives to vanquish its current unnatural condition.[19]

He continues by drawing out the continuity between natural human aspiration and the goal revealed and enabled by supernatural revelation and the faith attached to it:

[19] Ibid., p. 25.

Likewise, supernatural Revelation represents human nature's return to its authentic condition. At the same time it gives to it power to reach the final goal toward which it aspires. Likewise, supernatural Revelation confirms and recreates natural faith and nature itself as a mode of Revelation.[20]

So, Stăniloae sees the revealed Word engendering a renewed awareness and sense of its first communication as the creative Word. 'We do not know what nature itself fully is, nor the revelation it conveys except through the supernatural revelation.'[21] 'Only through the supernatural revelation do we fully know what nature, and the revelation it represents, are.' And this qualification of the former by the latter is crucial, says Stăniloae, since without the knowledge and power given in supernatural revelation the human person cannot engage the world in fulfillment of his or her aspiration for perfection and eternity.[22]

The argument in Chapter 2 takes up the relationship between natural revelation and supernatural in more detail, highlighting the universal, impersonal address of the former and the particular, personal address of the latter. Enough has been said, however, to show how Stăniloae views the world as a key source for his theology. The opening chapters of the *Dogmatic Theology* abundantly testify to the important place which human experience in and of the world occupies as a source for our reflection on the experience of God. The concern of subsequent chapters is an exploration of the place of creation, created existence and the natural order, within the Christian vision of God and his saving purposes. What part can the created human person, whether as an individual or in community, have in understanding and expressing that vision? In what way does theology reflect the essentially free character of a human person? And how is the freedom of theology balanced by responsibility, even accountability to the world which is so important a source for knowledge of God and encounters with God? Those are questions which we can now begin to explore.

---

[20] Ibid.
[21] Ibid., p. 25.
[22] Ibid., p. 30.

3

The Liturgy of the Mind: Dogma and Theology

A reader of Stăniloae's writings will be struck by the freedom of language and conceptualization that characterizes his thought. Such a freedom has its origin in two over-arching desires: first, to liberate Orthodox theology from all that prohibits it from becoming a genuinely universal expression of Christian faith; and second, to re-establish the link between theology and spirituality, to re-invest theology with an awareness of its spiritual consequences.[1] We need not look far in his *Dogmatic Theology* to discover ways in which Fr. Stăniloae has attempted to bring that creative vision to bear. His discussion of dogma and theology, for instance, in the first volume of the *Dogmatic Theology* witnesses to such an attempt. Within a larger discussion of 'Revelation: divine and ecclesial', which constitutes the introduction to his work, Stăniloae considers what Christians mean when they speak of dogma, and, following from that, what the relationship is between dogma and theology.[2]

---

[1] Bria, 'Vision,' 54–55.

[2] *DT*, I, p. 9–110. The nature of dogma *per se* is not a well-trodden path, as even Karl Rahner, writing from the Roman Catholic perspective, acknowledges. See his 'What Is a Dogmatic Statement?' in *Theological Investigations*, 23 vols. (London and New York, 1961–1992), vol. 5, p. 42.

In this chapter, then, I wish to investigate how Fr. Stăniloae understands and relates those two fundamental aspects of Christian believing. Obviously, the whole of his treatment cannot be described. Instead, I will draw upon the concluding portion of his discussion of 'ecclesial revelation' in which the character and relationship of dogma and theology are specifically considered.[3]

They are, of course, themes which we might expect at the beginning of a systematic exposition of Christian belief. But beyond that Stăniloae's exposition of dogma and theology offers insights which are especially pertinent for western Christian readers for whom the very notion of dogma can be troubling. After all, in our contemporary western theological context 'dogma' is often regarded as a negative, even stultifying factor in the life of faith and in the knowledge of God. Over thirty years ago Paul Tillich argued for the adoption of the phrase 'systematic theology' instead of 'dogmatic theology' on just those grounds. The words 'dogma' and 'dogmatic,' he argued, had been discredited to such a degree that their genuine meaning could not now be re-established.[4]

Whether the word or concept of dogma is as irretrievable as Tillich would have had us believe is uncertain. But if there is to be any rediscovery of the positive meaning of Christian dogma, it must, I think, be based upon an approach similar to that of Fr. Stăniloae. As we examine his understanding of dogma it is helpful to keep in mind how negative was the effect of his own first experience of traditional 'dogmatics' in his theological study. Perhaps for that reason especially Stăniloae's renewed commitment to the writing of dogmatic theology will aid us in rediscovering its positive meaning as a fundamental component of the Christian mind.

Revelation and Dogma

Our considerations must begin by noticing the context in which Stăniloae considers the nature of dogma and theology. Both

---

[3] *DT*, I, pp. 77–110.
[4] Paul Tillich, *Systematic Theology*, 3 vols. (Chicago, 1951–1963), vol. 1, p. 32.

are firmly set within his discussion of revelation. When all deference has been paid to the limitation of human, theological categories, Stăniloae nevertheless asserts a close coordination between revelation and dogma, between the divine and the human in the apprehension of the reality of God. It is, I think, helpful to recall here a distinction that the Russian exile theologian Georges Florovsky made from a more historical point of view. For Florovsky, kerygma and dogma are not to be regarded as separable components of Christian experience but rather as two 'basic stages' in the proclamation of the Gospel.[5] Even if a chronological distinction must be made between the two, in the continuing life of the church such a distinction diminishes in significance. Describing what he considered to be the genuine character of patristic theology (significantly, he refuses to restrict the designation 'patristic' to any historical era), Florovsky explained:

> There are two basic stages in the proclamation of the Christian faith. *Our simple faith had to acquire composition.* There was an inner urge, an inner logic, an internal necessity, in this transition – from *kerygma* to *dogma.* Indeed, the *dogmata* of the Fathers are essentially the same 'simple' *kerygma* . . . But now it is – this very *kerygma* – properly articulated and developed into a consistent body of correlated testimonies.[6]

By locating his discussion of dogma within the framework of revelation Stăniloae attempts to make the same assertion from a more strictly theological perspective. For when he describes the content of dogma as 'doctrinal expressions of the plan for salvation revealed and realized in Christ' he intends just such a continuity between revelation and dogma.[7]

How is such a close alignment of revelation and dogma possible? For Stăniloae, it is only possible by means of a pneumatological understanding of the church. The church which 'preserves, preaches, applies or fructifies, explicates and defines' dogma is not conceived of in static, institutional terms,

---

[5] Georges Florovsky, *Aspects* (Belmont, 1975), p. 16.
[6] Ibid.; italics are his.
[7] *DT*, p. 71.

but as a community of persons 'who believe in Christ and who
have taken their being from the descent of the Spirit and from
the apostolic preaching of Christ.'[8] Its permanent pentecostal
character means that the church is itself part of the revelatory
action of God. It is continuously called into being by the
active 'pressure' of the Spirit of divine personal disclosure,
one that evokes a similar, responsive disclosure from us. The
Spirit constantly re-creates the church through continuous
divine self-disclosure which in turn evokes humanity's
response. Such self-disclosure is the substance of God's
revelation. This is what Fr. Stăniloae means when he says that
'the Holy Spirit maintains the Church by holding in evidence
continuously the very same effective presence of Christ.'[9] He
continues:

> The Revelation remains effective through the Church; the
> Church is the medium of the Revelation's continued efficacy. The
> Church vivifies the Revelation; the Revelation vivifies the Church.
> In this way the Revelation assumes an ecclesial aspect, and its
> expressions and dogmas become expressions and dogmas of the
> Church.[10]

The revelation and its continuing effect in calling people to faith
is wrought by the Spirit. Within this strongly pneumatological
understanding of the church as the context of the continuous
divine disclosure Stăniloae locates the character and purpose
of dogma.

A Personalist Approach to Knowing God

In his discussion of dogma Fr. Stăniloae challenges us to adjust
our entire approach. Through the co-ordination of revelation
and dogma the character of dogma is determined primarily by
the personal quality of God's self-disclosure. The same personal
character of divine self-disclosure determines the way in which
we comprehend and appropriate it. Therefore, Stăniloae's

---

[8] Ibid., p. 75.
[9] Ibid., p. 76.
[10] Ibid.

approach to dogma is not historical-critical; not based, that is, upon a concept of human knowing which, following the popular approach of the 'scientific method,' simply searches for an 'objective' truth or meaning that inheres in the object of study regardless of our understanding or encounter with it. Rather, Stăniloae insists, dogma must be understood personalistically, that is, after the fashion of the disclosure of one person to another.

His own characteristic description of God as 'eternal' or 'infinite' Person, which we encountered in the previous chapter, means that God is not closed in upon himself. Consequently, God is not an object of rational speculation but one encountered in an act of personal communion.[11] That refusal to objectivize God is fundamental to Stăniloae's approach. He insists that God can never be 'object.' Indeed, the revelation of God as Trinity precludes such objectivization.[12] As 'infinite Person' God is always 'subject', whose infinity signifies engagement with an unbounded multiplicity of human subjects. Knowledge between God and humankind is mediated through mutual communication, an ongoing dialogue between divine and human subjects.[13]

Stăniloae's characteristic use of terms such as 'communication' and 'dialogue', arising from his personalistic approach, parallels important trends in contemporary western treatments of epistemology. Hans-Georg Gadamer, for example, in his *Truth and Method*, employs conversational parallels to describe various modes of knowing. The most profound kind of human knowing is likened to conversation which involves a recognition of the claim of one speaker upon the other. It involves, in

[11] *DT*, I, pp. 77–79.

[12] See his discussion of the Trinity, *DT*, I, pp. 300–364. A similar though complex discussion in English can be found in his essay 'The Holy Trinity: Structure of Supreme Love,' in *Theology and the Church*, trans. Robert Barringer (Crestwood, 1980), pp. 73–108.

[13] The significance of Christ as *Logos*, the Word, is that 'in Christ God gives himself as hypostasis [person]. In Christ the divine hypostasis becomes accessible for full communion' (*Dieu est Amour* [Genève, 1980], p. 63). The section, 'l'éternité', pp. 48–68, is generally relevant to the theme of person, communion and knowledge.

other words, an existential openness.[14] The same kind of knowing is operative in the sphere of divine revelation. Working from our human experience, Stăniloae observes:

> Once the existence of a person has been revealed to me, that person becomes, in a way, the purpose of my existence; he becomes for me the proof, the truth of yet another level of existence in so far as I am no more able to understand the purpose of my existence apart from that person.[15]

The knowledge of persons as subjects has to do not simply with awareness but with engagement. It is what Kierkegaard described as 'subjective truth,' meaning not that such knowledge is, as Andrew Louth puts it, 'a collection of subjective impressions,' but that its significance lies in the subject's engagement with it.[16] Stăniloae suggests this too when he comments that 'if a man does not wish to exist *for* another person, he does not exist *to* other persons.'[17]

The revelation of one person to another person is founded upon engagement and self-disclosure. Here again, what is true of communication between persons is, for Stăniloae, pre-eminently true between God, the infinite Person, and all human persons. So, he says,

> A person does not reveal himself, that is, he does not disclose himself except to him who opens himself to such a disclosure. As a relationship between persons this holds true with respect to revelation. A person does not disclose himself to me unless I disclose myself to him. How much more this is true of the divine Person.[18]

Just as the divine revelation depends upon the human disclosure in faith or trust, so too dogma, as a means of the

---

[14] Here I am following Andrew Louth's analysis in *Discerning the Mystery. An essay on the nature of theology* (Oxford, 1983), p. 41. The second and third chapters of Louth's study have been especially helpful to me in focusing some of the implicit or presumed elements in Fr. Stăniloae's presentation.

[15] *DT*, I, p. 73.
[16] Louth, p. 27.
[17] *DT*, I, p. 74; italics mine.
[18] Ibid., p. 73.

effective extension of the divine revelation within the life of the church and the experience of believers, must elicit a similar responsive disclosure or openness by believers if it is to be understood and engaged.[19]

Living Dogma

This approach to dogma is emphasized by Stăniloae's evaluation of Christ within the dogmatic scheme. Far from being a system of learning, dogma is nothing less than 'the translation of the reality of Christ as it is directed toward men.'[20] More particularly that reality is 'the plan of deification' for the cosmos fully accomplished in Christ.[21] 'In Christ', says Stăniloae,

> is concentrated and realized all that is expressed in Christian dogmas: there is expressed the divine infinity in which his human nature participates and in which everything else, through his common human nature, has power to participate.[22]

And so the model of Christian dogma, its content and purpose, is Christ. Christ himself, he affirms, is 'living dogma.'[23]

In seeking after a unified dogmatic system we must not, Fr. Stăniloae contends, strive for an arrangement 'on the basis of abstract principles,' but rather look to 'the living unity of Christ.'[24] The 'living unity' found in Christ is mutuality of life. That, he believes, is the foundational theme that unites all Christian dogma. He describes this mutuality as 'the movement to a communion ever more intimate between us and the personal God.'[25] The mystery of Christ is the mystery of humanity in communion with the infinity of God. This is the truth to which classical christology points; it is also, Stăniloae claims, the distillation of the Gospel revelation itself.

[19] Ibid., pp. 74, 77.
[20] Ibid., p. 79.
[21] Ibid.
[22] Ibid.
[23] Ibid.
[24] Ibid., p. 78.
[25] Ibid. p. 79.

But the mystery of Christ as the consummate expression in time and space of mutuality of life extends beyond Christ. For if the incarnate Christ is the living expression of all dogma then this same Incarnation has the power to draw us into the depths of its own source and paradigm, the Holy Trinity, the 'communion of perfect love.'[26] Stăniloae's appeal to the Trinity as well as to the Incarnation in the understanding of dogma highlights the coinherence of those two truths within the economy of salvation. Christ reveals the 'eternal community' of the Trinity, and his saving action also leads believers into communion with the Trinity, 'the structure of perfect community.'[27]

Stăniloae's interest is to help us see that the two coinhering realities of Trinity and Incarnation are not simply objects of faith, truths which we believe or to which we give intellectual assent, nor are they merely components, albeit primary ones, of a series of dogmatic formulas. They are part of the ground of faith; they embody and express the meaning of faith understood principally as *trust*. In presenting to us the meaning of person and communion – or, better, personal communion, communion between persons – they draw us back to the fundamental Gospel faith. That faith, understood as trust, is self-disclosure to God in response to his own personal self-disclosure to us, and then our consequential self-disclosure to other human persons.

Stăniloae regards such an understanding of dogma as a fundamental source of Christian liberty. It has already been suggested how the apprehension of dogma presumes a free and personal response of self-disclosure. In addition, it holds before the believer a horizon of infinite development or infinite extension toward the infinity of God the 'infinite Person.' Jesus Christ, 'living dogma,' is the one in whom this progression is complete before us. Christ, precisely because he is both God and man, is the one through whom such a progression is possible for us.[28] Therefore the dogmatic vision is inherently

---

[26] Ibid.
[27] Ibid., p. 80.
[28] Ibid., p. 96.

dynamic and progressive, and, most important of all, it has spiritual consequences. When properly situated within the life of the church, dogma helps to maintain the purity of the Gospel by continually redirecting Christians to the Gospel's fundamental challenge. In contrast to the perennial temptation to reduce the Gospel to a frame of mind or an ethic, the dogmas of the Trinity and the Incarnation, and, by implication, all dogmas that flow from them and lead back to them, confront us with the irreducible Gospel challenge of trust. They mean to elicit our full and potentially eternal personhood by reshaping our existence in terms of the human content of trust: communion, self-disclosure and mutuality of life. To invoke and to explore Christian dogma as a window onto the reality of God is, from Stăniloae's perspective, to invoke and explore the reality of love which is the expression of trust, communion and exchange between persons. For Stăniloae, therefore, the Johannine affirmation is pre-eminent: 'God is love' (1 Jn. 4.8). Only when we see love there do we truly know any and every dogma. Only then do we see how the dogmas of the church are necessary for our salvation. Only then do they fulfil their purpose in intensifying the Gospel light by which we discern our eternal destiny in the triune God.

Dogma and Theology

As foundational expressions of all that dogma means, Incarnation and Trinity guide the relationship between dogma and theology. Here too Stăniloae finds the relationship between dogma and theology helped by a personalistic parallel. In this parallel the trinitarian and christological dynamic of unity in multiplicity prevails. Such a 'paradox,' he claims, characterizes all genuine personhood since for Stăniloae a person is 'a unity, but one of infinite richness; the same, yet infinite in variety and newness in its expressions and circumstances.'[29] Indeed, everything in which personhood is involved reveals a similar paradox. And so, he says of inter-personal relations: 'Man is autonomous and yet he is not able to have life, nor can he realize

[29] Ibid.

himself, except in community with others.'[30] Likewise, in a person's interaction with the world, he 'embraces the world in all its variety, drawing it into unity, and yet he remains distinctly unique while the world is maintained in its variety.' 'How much more inevitable,' he concludes, 'is such a paradox in the relations of the infinite God with the limited created world.'[31]

In understanding the relationship between dogma and theology, then, we must bear in mind the infinite content of dogmas which, like the divine infinity of Christ and the Trinity whose presence they bear, is apprehended only through the window of human particularity and finitude. Stăniloae writes beautifully of this interaction of infinity and particularity:

> God in himself is a mystery. Of his inner existence nothing can be said. But through creation, through providence and his work of salvation, God comes down to the level of man. He who has made us thinking and speaking beings has made himself accessible to our thought and our speech. Touching our spirit he awakens in us thoughts and words which convey the experience of his encounter with us. But at the same time we realize that our thoughts and our words about him do not contain him completely as he is in himself. For us men they are flowers grown up from the depths of his ineffable mystery. Our words and thoughts of God are both cataphatic and apophatic, that is, they say some-thing and yet at the same time they suggest the ineffable. If we remain enclosed within our formulae they become idols; if we reject any and every formula we drown in the undefined chaos of that ocean. Our words and thoughts are a finite opening towards the infinite, transparencies for the infinite, so they are able to foster within us a spiritual life.[32]

Here the correlation between dogma and theology is suggested. Theology is unceasing reflection upon the all-encompassing and infinite content lying within, communic-able through, dogmatic formulations. It follows from his

[30] Ibid.
[31] Ibid.
[32] Stăniloae, *Theology and the Church*, p. 73.

personalistic paradigm of unity and multiplicity that the conceptualizations of earlier Christian epochs which have become dogmas should never be lifeless fragments. Rather, such dogmas are meant to be a gateway through which we pass into the 'unfathomed richness' of the triune God's 'inexpressible depth and complexity.'[33] There exists, therefore, a necessary and creative mutuality between the church's tradition of dogmatic formulation and its ongoing theological reflection. 'The faithful,' Stăniloae insists,

> cannot be satisfied with the repetition of outlines of the dogmas; they must endeavour to enter into their endless depth, aided by an understanding founded upon holy Scripture and holy Tradition. Theology is, therefore, a necessity implicit in the Church's need to explicate to believers the points of faith.[34]

Far from being static, theology is necessarily dynamic. It emerges out of the creative impact of Christian kerygma and dogma in each generation. As such, it is to be done by every member of the church everywhere.

An Intellectual Liturgy

Because in the Orthodox Church the language of the church's dogmatic tradition pervades its liturgical life, prayer and worship form the context in which this particular interaction of dogma and theology is based. Stăniloae quotes the famous phrase of Evagrius of Pontus (AD 346–399): '. . . he who prays truly is a theologian; and he who is a theologian truly prays.'[35] Theology is the attempt by human persons to know divine, infinite Person as the mystery of that divine personhood relates *to our particular circumstances*. It is the dogmatic reality as it is shaped by the specific context of an individual and a community. The theologian, he says,

> seeks to know God through the experience of God's saving work toward humankind. Yet he cannot know this salvation unless he

---

[33] *DT*, I, p. 96.
[34] Ibid., p. 93.
[35] Ibid., p. 101.

enters into a personal rapport of love with God and the faithful through prayer.[36]

Theology becomes what Ion Bria, describing Stăniloae's vision, calls 'an intellectual liturgy,' a form of doxology whose symbolic language evokes the language of prayer.[37]

It is significant that Stăniloae qualifies this appeal to encounter with God in prayer by situating such prayer within the wider life of the prayer of all the faithful. It is not just in prayer but also 'in cult,' that is, in liturgical worship, in the church's authentic spirituality, where the church's 'living dialogue with Christ' is found.[38] It is verified not simply in the solitary prayer of the individual. 'Theology is much more that which is prayed with other members of the Church,'[39] he affirms. Moreover, to the extent that the theologian's own dialogue of prayer complements and enhances this communal dialogue, his personal theological reflections or insights assume significance within believers' ongoing life of witness and sanctification. Such liturgical prayer, as the recurrent expression and experience of our mutual love before God, leads the theologian more certainly toward the discovery of God's saving love for him.[40] Also, the basis of theological reflection within a corporate life of prayer and worship sets that reflection more securely within the framework of the church's common, inherited teaching. This helps to counteract the desire for originality at any price which Stăniloae regards as specially destructive to theology's corporate responsibility.

Theology's rootedness in the church's liturgical life is part of that process whereby theologians penetrate to the mystery of Christ, the living dogma, so that they might witness to it in their own time and circumstance. Like dogma, the liturgy

[36] Ibid., p. 102.

[37] Bria, 'Vision,' 55. Such an understanding of theology is becoming more widespread among western theologians. See, for instance, the work of Methodist Geoffrey Wainwright, *Doxology, The Praise of God in Worship, Doctrine and Life: A Systematic Theology* (London, 1980).

[38] *DT*, I, p. 101.

[39] Ibid., p. 102.

[40] Ibid.

draws us into the tension of paradox. Fixed in the particularity of our earthly situation, indeed, deriving its effective symbols from that very created particularity, it is nevertheless transparent, directing our vision toward the eschatological horizon of God's unbounded infinity. It is the place where dogma becomes experience because it is the place where Christ is experienced as present and active in sign, symbol, kerygma and sacrament. For the theologian there can be little fidelity to the church's dogmatic tradition, little appreciation of its role as a window through which we peer into divine Person's unfathomable depth, unless it is experienced within the ongoing life of the liturgical tradition where its metaphorical and symbolic quality and power are secure. Theology is always doxological.[41] There the liturgies not only of the human intellect, but of the human heart and body are united in the worship of Christ, the living dogma, in whom true theology has its beginning and end.[42]

'Secular' Theology

If this is the ground out of which a 'living theology' arises, what are the marks of such a theology? According to Fr. Stăniloae the progress of theology is bound to three inter-related factors. First, 'faithfulness to the revelation in Christ handed on in Holy Scripture, Holy Tradition, and lived without interruption in the life of the Church;' second, 'responsibility to the faithful of the age in which theology is being done;' and finally, openness to our 'eschatological life,' by which he means 'the obligation to set believers on the path toward their fulfillment in the life to come.'[43] All three characteristics must inhere at one and the same time if the theology of any one person or any one period is to be true to its task. Failure to fulfil any one of those conditions produces a theology that is not only 'insufficient' and 'useless,' but more than that, even 'injurious' to believers.[44]

[41] See Wainwright's work, cited in note 37, for a systematic development of this theme in current western theology.

[42] *DT*, I, p. 102.

[43] Ibid., p. 105.

[44] Ibid., p. 104.

While the danger of theology being trapped in the formulas of a system is constant, equally constant is its need to be what Stăniloae calls a 'secular' theology. He means a theology which gives whole-hearted attention to the proper value and progress of the age (*saeculum*):

> Like it or not [he says] theology is immeasurably bound in its different periods to the conceptualizations of those periods. Therefore, the fixing upon conceptualizations that have lost their value with the passing of the period from which they were taken and the desire to maintain such concepts permanently as a basis of theology, make the formulas of that theology into lifeless fragments, foreign to the life of the Church as well as to the believers of succeeding generations.[45]

To the degree that any theology is content with a literal repetition of words or formulas of the past it is insufficient.[46] The 'infidelity' of such theology is three-fold: toward the unlimited character of revelation: toward theology's contemporary milieu: and toward the eschatological future toward which all things progress.

Nevertheless, as we saw earlier, dogmatic formulas of previous, even distant, ages can have positive and enduring value for the church's understanding and proclamation of the Gospel. Such, Stăniloae believes, are the classic patristic formulas expressing the Trinity and the Incarnation: three persons in one nature and two natures in one person. Stăniloae's own interpretation of those terms exemplifies their enduring significance for the theologian. His appeal to them is motivated not by the erroneous belief that they are definitive explanations of the

---

[45] Ibid.

[46] Such theology, 'trapped in the formulas of the past,' Stăniloae admits, was characteristic of much Orthodox theology well into this century. Reflecting on that situation, he notes: 'This was a theology that impeded every spiritual awakening and every impulse of the Spirit. It lost all sense of dynamism by reflecting a static, external order that believed itself to be perfect. This signifies a lack of responsibility toward the faithful of its respective age and, therefore, toward the obligation to work for the religious awakening of its age. This, in turn, points to a failure of responsibility in the face of the richness and profundity of the Revelation as it is expressed in Holy Scripture and in the apostolic and patristic tradition.' Ibid.

reality to which they bear witness. Even in their original context they did not do that.[47] They are valuable because of what we might call their evocative power. Their situation within the church's life of prayer and worship, their communal invocation and affirmation by the multiplicity of believers, their association with the sacramental mystery of human particularity opening onto divine infinity, maintain the meanings of these words as experienceable realities. These formulas are most readily transparent to the mystery which is God; they are, as Michael Polanyi might say, most easily seen through.[48]

The inadequacy of such formulas on the philosophical level compels us to approach them from another point of view. We must seek to penetrate through them into an experience of personal disclosure before God and one another. In this way they aid us to enter into the mystery of God, that is, the mystery of divine Person. That involves trust, communion and love. In this way the theologian is made ready to explicate and 'fructify' the meaning of the dogmas through his theological reflection in words, images or concepts that impact dynamically in his or her own time and circumstance.

The Virtues of Theology

Returning, then, to the three marks of genuine theology, Fr. Stăniloae describes them as apostolic, contemporary, and prophetic-eschatological. In its apostolicity theology must be faithful to the witness of Christ as the definitive revelation of God. In Christ the fundamental anchor for our understanding of God is given.[49] At the same time, it must be contemporary. A truly contemporary theology aids in a practical way man's present spiritual pilgrimage toward communion with God and with others. Stăniloae describes the positive meaning of such a contemporary theology by affirming that it gives whole-hearted attention to the *saeculum*, in the sense that it observes the

---

[47] See John Meyendorff, *Christ in Eastern Christian Thought* (Crestwood, 1975), p. 28.

[48] See Louth's discussion, *Discerning*, pp. 61ff.

[49] *DT*, I, p. 108.

consistency and value of the world, and must help the world's true development toward that which constitutes genuine Christian humanity.[50] And then, theology must be prophetic and eschatological. It must be a theology that challenges the world to conformity to the risen Christ while reminding the world that this goal is a gift from beyond time and space, something unattainable fully within the historical process. In this third characteristic we can perhaps see most clearly the way in which Stăniloae's understanding of the task of theology has been developed in reaction to the Marxist ideology amidst which, until the end of his life, he lived. Theology's prophetic-eschatological character is, he would contend, still universally applicable. At the very least, it encourages a dynamic theology, one that beckons all things on to final transfiguration in God's love.

The power and virtue of genuine theology, he believes, consists of faith, love and hope, the so-called theological virtues (1 Cor. 13.13). 'Through faith,' he says,

> it manifests the real revelation of God in Christ; through love it discloses to believers the perspective of the complete appro-priation of the riches made known in Christ; through love it enables the faithful to achieve union now with Christ as well as with one another . . . through hope comes the disclosure of a future of total participation in the wealth of Christ and a leading onward toward him . . .[51]

As a liturgy of the mind linked with our spiritual progress toward the Kingdom, theology participates in the movement of the human spirit toward complete communion with God.[52] The proper and positive value of Christian dogmas and the theology they generate depends upon an apprehension of their meaning within the context of prayer. They are, as it were, the sacramental food for the liturgy of our minds even as bread and wine are the sacramental food for the liturgy of our souls and bodies.

---

[50] Ibid., p. 105.
[51] Ibid., p. 107.
[52] Ibid., p. 109.

The understanding of dogma and theology in Fr. Stăniloae's *Orthodox Dogmatic Theology* witnesses to the possibility of a dogmatic commitment which is open and creative *because* it is rooted in the experience of Christ, who is the personal embodiment of the mystery of God, and humankind. To that experience dogma irrevocably points. In the face of dogmatism, on the one hand, and the acids of scepticism,[53] on the other, Christians need not apologize for their dogmatic tradition. It challenges them to a love which is never content to remain where it is, but must by its very nature delve always more deeply into the mystery of the God who can be known in so far as he is loved and in so far as we, who seek to know him, love one another.

[53] So Hugh Montefiore regarding the present intellectual climate in *Christian Believing: the Nature of the Christian Faith and Its Expression in Holy Scripture and Creeds* (London, 1976), p. 40.

4

Rediscovering Cosmic Christianity

The rediscovery of a Christianity in which God, humankind and the whole created order are given their proper value and are seen in their mutual interdependence is, Stăniloae insists, one of the urgent tasks of contemporary theology:

> Christianity must emphasize today the value and the mystery of man and the world in a special way, in order to save man from a grave moral decadence and a remarkable egoism in interhuman relations; and to save the world from total catastrophe.[1]

Owing to advances in scientific knowledge and technological expertise we experience now more acutely than ever before the choice between blessing and curse, between life and death. It is a concern which is rapidly becoming central to theological reflection at the global level. Stăniloae's reflections, of course, pre-date heightened ecological awareness in the West. Their context was post-war Romania where industrialization was ruthless and, as we now know, often ecologically and humanly devastating. Just because Stăniloae's theology of creation is so naturally integrated into his theological vision it may provide other Christians with useful insights for developing a Christian

---

[1] Beauregard, p. 47.

vision of the world, components for a viable cosmology and ecology. In his exposition of this very theme, in fact, Dumitru Stăniloae's theology is said to be most prophetic,[2] while developing sometimes forgotten emphases from his own eastern Christian tradition. Stăniloae's theology of the created order embodies in an exemplary way his belief in the irrepressible richness of theology as it seeks to be faithful at one and the same time to past, present and future.

There are several aspects of Fr. Stăniloae's theology of creation that have impressed his readers. Some, for instance, have found his theology of space and time, to be especially insightful.[3] I wish to focus upon his theology of the natural world and its specific relation to humankind since here more than elsewhere, I think, we can see how he endeavours to bring the insights of his Romanian Orthodox religious tradition to bear in a fruitful way upon our modern 'culture of technology.'[4] It takes us directly to Stăniloae's understanding of the world as gift.

Our Solidarity with the Creation

Even the cursory reader will easily detect the formative influence upon Stăniloae's thought of the theology of Maximus the Confessor. From him, together with the Greek fathers generally, he appropriated the themes of the creative *Logos*, the created *logoi*, and cosmic transfiguration.[5] Those are themes which any discussion of Stăniloae's theology of the world must consider. But even at the more fundamental level concerned with the character of revelation we have seen how Stăniloae echoes Maximus for whom, he says, 'any essential distinction' between natural revelation and supernatural or

[2] Clément, p. 17.
[3] Daniel Neeser, 'The World: Gift of God and Scene of Humanity's Response,' *The Ecumenical Review*, 33, no. 3 (1981): 272–282; Clément, pp. 17–18.
[4] The phrase is Arnold Pacey's, *The Culture of Technology* (Cambridge, USA, 1983).
[5] See the comments of John Meyendorff in his Preface to Stăniloae's *Theology and the Church*, p. 9; likewise, Clément, p. 17.

biblical revelation is to be rejected.[6] Much of what Fr. Stăniloae says, therefore, about the natural world and humanity's place within it must be set within those insights inherited from the Greek patristic and Byzantine traditions.

In his understanding of the natural order Stăniloae stresses the 'solidarity' between humankind and the natural world. It has been observed that some of the most beautiful passages in his *Orthodox Dogmatic Theology* concern just this relationship.[7] The source of that solidarity is the part which the natural order is meant to play in God's acts of self-disclosure. Fundamentally it means that the created world around us is not to be engaged simply as the incidental, unrelated context of man's life and spiritual growth. Rather, it means, on the one hand, that the natural order has a chief part to play in man's sanctification and deification, and, on the other hand, that the created world derives its primary meaning from its part in humankind's salvific progress.[8] So there exists a profound bond between humankind and the natural order. It is not a relationship of dominion and subjection, as Genesis 1.28 has often been read, but of mutual need, responsibility and interdependence.

Reference has already been made to Stăniloae's appeal to Maximus's notion of man as *microcosm* and the world as *macanthropos*.[9] Developing a theme that has its origins at least as far back as Gregory of Nyssa (*c.*330–*c.*395) Maximus expounds the theme that humanity's movement Godward possesses cosmic impact. Because man is a microcosm, a bridge-figure poised between the visible and invisible worlds and comprehending within himself characteristics of both, he is also a mediator. And so, says another commentator on Maximus's insight, 'man finds God in the world and the world needs man in order to find its Creator again.'[10] Owing to this interaction, even the eternal destinies of both can be similarly described. Stăniloae, therefore, echoes Maximus when he speaks of the

[6] *DT*, I, p. 9.
[7] Neeser, 275.
[8] *DT*, I, pp. 323–328.
[9] For its use in Maximus, see, for instance, *Ep.* 6, *PG* 91:429D.
[10] John Meyendorff, *Christ in Eastern Christian Thought* (Crestwood, 1975), p. 139.

world as a work of God's love destined for deification.[11] As a consequence of these influences Stăniloae avoids the tendency in much western theology to individualize the process of human salvation to such an extent that it is separated from the wider and sustaining context of human life, the world. Another important qualification follows as well. Despite Stăniloae's stress upon the existential rootedness of dogma and theology which the previous chapter highlighted, Maximus's influence allows him to correct the tendencies of much existentialist theology in which this unfortunate divorce has been so prominent.[12] Such a divide, Stăniloae maintains, flies in the face of our common experience:

> Nature appears very clearly as the medium through which man is able to do good or ill to himself, either developing or degenerating from an ethical or spiritual point of view. Nature is plainly involved in inter-human dialogue – be it beneficial or destructive – without which neither the individual nor the community can exist.[13]

The ethical and spiritual development for which the created world is the inevitable medium is nothing less than the sanctification and deification of man. Says Stăniloae, 'God seeks to make himself known to man in love, to provide the context for a relationship in which full participation in his life, full communion with him, becomes possible.'[14]

The World as Gift

Upon the basis of such an integrated vision of Christ, humanity and the natural world, Fr. Stăniloae develops his distinctive theology of the world as *gift*. Whenever he speaks of 'gift' we must understand that it signifies less a thing than a process of

---

[11] *DT, I*, p. 323–324.

[12] Ibid., p. 323. In this regard he makes specific reference to the school of thought inspired by the German existentialist New Testament scholar and theologian Rudolph Bultmann (1884–1976). It lacked, Stăniloae thought, any serious theology of the created world.

[13] Ibid., p. 324.

[14] Ibid., p. 338.

personal interaction and disclosure. Stăniloae attempts to convey this dynamic character by his phrase, 'the dialogue of the gift.'[15] When we receive a gift from someone we are meant to fix our awareness not on the gift but on the giver.[16] The genuine 'dialogue of the gift' requires more than simple acknowledgement, though; it must evoke an exchange of gifts which finally should be nothing less than mutual movement of two persons toward one another. When properly experienced, then, a gift always points beyond itself. It becomes a means of personal communication and self-disclosure. This 'dialogue of the gift' is, as he says elsewhere, a 'dialogue of love.' And so, the meaning and purpose of the gift is discovered in its being transcended in a communion of love.[17] This same understanding of gift applies at the cosmic level to the purpose of the world in the relationship between God and humankind.

As the medium for such a 'dialogue of the gift' the world is much more than an impersonal context of divine-human communication. Instead, it is the very stuff of the 'dialogue of love' between God and us. In its quality as gift, therefore, the world attains to a centrality in that process whereby humanity experiences personal communion with God, supreme Person.

This 'dialogue of the gift' has its first utterance in the creation of the world by the Word, when God gave it as a gift to humanity. From the beginning, in fact, the world has assumed the character of a word and is meant to be 'God's coherent conversation with man.'[18] By continually sustaining the world in existence God is renewing, reinitiating his part in the dialogue.

Yet as has already been observed, this 'dialogue of the gift' depends upon mutuality and reciprocity if it is to be purposeful. To God's creative initiative humankind must respond. God's gift of the world is not merely to sustain us by being received,

[15] Ibid., p. 341.
[16] For a devotional exposition of this theme see *Victory*, pp. 5ff.
[17] Ibid.
[18] *DT*, I, p. 340.

it is intended to draw us into dialogue, to become a means of spiritual growth by providing humanity with a reciprocal gift for God.[19]

Humanity's Natural Priesthood

Within the context of this 'dialogue of the gift' and its attendant demand for a reciprocal gift from humanity Stăniloae invokes the theme of our natural priesthood. This natural priesthood is a vocation inherent in the call to mastery over the created world given at the time of our creation (Gen. 1.28). Through its innate priestly character humankind is enabled to present the world as a gift back to God. In that way it enters into the dialogue of the gift and expresses its communion with God. But how is humankind to do this? What gift can humanity return to God?

The exercise of this natural priesthood in returning a gift to God is made possible, first of all, by the character of the natural world itself. Far from being static or inert, the natural world is malleable to an almost infinite degree. 'Nature,' Stăniloae writes, 'is manifested as a plastic rationality which can, in principle, be modelled without limit by the human consciousness.'[20] Nature becomes the medium in which humanity grows spiritually when we comprehend, shape and bring to fruition its 'unlimited potentiality.'[21] For this reason Fr. Stăniloae looks very positively on the contributions of modern science since they have revealed more fully than ever before the plasticity of the cosmos. The many new discoveries of nature's hitherto undefined potentials resulting from scientific enquiry are themselves part of the exercise of this natural priesthood and so should be seen as a positive component of our spiritual pilgrimage and growth into Christlikeness.

Likewise, the application of those discoveries through technology is to be regarded as another dimension of the

[19] Ibid.
[20] Ibid., p. 327.
[21] Ibid., p. 325.

exercise of natural priesthood. Indeed, the legitimate physical and spiritual needs of humankind demand that nature be reshaped to meet those needs through 'a continually creative imagination.'[22]

Here it is necessary to recall again the influence of Maximus the Confessor and his doctrine of the creative *Logos* and created *logoi*.[23] Building upon themes in Alexandrian theology, Maximus sees the *logoi* not only as the defining and unifying factor in all created things, but also as embodying their divine purpose within the divine *Logos* himself.[24] Each person, uniquely called to share in the image and likeness of Christ the *Logos*, possesses at least in part the *Logos's* power of unifying the infinite *logoi* according to their divinely established purpose, the 'ordering and unifying task' that man's mediatorial role accords him.[25] For Maximus all that exists is a materialization or, as Stăniloae puts it, a 'plasticization' of the many *logoi* radiating from the *Logos*.[26] Created as we are in the image of the personal *Logos*, each of us is called to penetrate the natural order so as to decipher the manifold ways in which it reflects and so *reveals* the *Logos* by whom it was created. 'Only in man,' therefore, 'does the rationality of nature's undefined potentials obtain a meaning, a purpose; only in him does it progress ever more deeply toward its fulfillment.'[27]

Although Stăniloae has developed this notion of the plasticity of the created order and its openness to a unifying mind and purpose outside itself apart from the discussions between the philosophers of science and theologians here in the West, it is notable how compatible his insights are with current discussions of cosmology from the theological and scientific angles. The *Logos/logoi* theme, for instance, expresses the two-fold characteristics of regularity or order and freedom or openness which modern physicists tell us is the real dynamic within the created order. And the notion of the plasticity of the creation is

[22] Ibid., p. 326.
[23] See Thunberg, *Microcosm*, pp. 67–69, 76–84; and *Man, passim*.
[24] Ibid., pp. 68, 79.
[25] Ibid., p. 147.
[26] *DT*, I, p. 327.
[27] Ibid., p. 345.

consistent with their suggestion that physical process is ontologically open.[28]

These innumerable 'undefined potentials' are not to be discovered for their own sakes alone. The positive significance of the world's plasticity is only experienced when the under-lying unity of the *Logos*, Christ, is discerned there. Such a discernment occurs when nature is 'guided and used in conformity with its inherent purpose,' that is, when 'beneficial designs' issue for the larger human community while at the same time directing the human community's awareness Godward.[29] Here we glimpse the pertinence of this world view for contemporary economics, science and technology. The genuine exercise of natural priesthood, 'mastery' properly understood, is so constituted. Such mastery can become domination, however, by a refusal to respect nature's purpose in God. When man 'sterilizes, poisons and abuses' creation he not only works against greater human solidarity but by that same fact impedes his spiritual growth.[30] As is the case for personal existence so too for the natural order, meaning is found in the experience of solidarity between persons which trinitarian life implies.

When this uniquely human creative mastery is properly exercised, Stăniloae believes, it provides men and women with their gifts and thus enables them to express their part in the dialogue of the gift. So, says Stăniloae,

> . . . the gifts given to us by God can become our gifts to God through the fact that we are free to give things back to God. We transform things into our gifts by the exercise of our freedom and by the love which we show to God. Toward this end we are able to transform and combine them endlessly. God has given the world to man not only as a gift of continuous fruitfulness, but as one immensely rich in possible alterations, actualized by each person through freedom and labour. This actualization, like the multiplication of talents given by God, is the gift of humankind to God.[31]

---

[28] See John Polkinghorne, *Reason and Reality. The Relationship Between Science and Theology* (London, 1991), pp. 83 and 42.

[29] *DT*, I, p. 325.

[30] Ibid.

[31] Ibid., p. 341.

Priestly Labour

Within such a scheme human labour in all its varied expressions assumes theological and spiritual importance. Here perhaps more than anywhere else we see how Fr. Stăniloae attempts to meet in a positive way the challenges of marxist ideology in which man, the *homo sovieticus* of then current political ideology, is regarded primarily as 'the worker' whose task is to transform and humanize nature by his labour.[32]

In contrast to one long-standing perspective within the Christian tradition which sees human labour as a consequence of man's estrangement from God and so as a largely negative factor in human experience, Fr. Stăniloae is anxious to re-establish labour as something spiritually valuable, positive, even joyful.[33] Thought, imagination and physical labour all contribute to the transformation of the natural world into human gifts to God. It is an essential part of the dialogue of the gift that lies at the heart of man's proper relationship to the natural order and is one way in which the world's potential sacramentality begins to be realized. For Stăniloae the sacraments are the paradigm for this free gift-giving:

> . . . no one returns to God the things he has received without his own labour being added to them. Grapes, bread, wine, oil given to God – they are not only gifts to God but things imprinted with human labour.[34]

[32] Georgescu, *Romanians*, p. 234. Because of the political circumstances in which he wrote any evaluation of Stăniloae's attempts to challenge marxist ideology must be read between the lines. Undoubtedly, it would be an immensely fruitful object of further study. Some preliminary comparisons can be made, though, on the basis of Paul Oestreicher's essay 'Marxism, Nature and Work,' in Hugh Montefiore, ed., *Man and Nature* (London, 1975), pp. 169–179.

[33] It is interesting to compare Stăniloae's theology of labour with another treatment arising out of dialogue with, in part, marxist ideology, that of Pope John Paul II, *On Human Work* [Encyclical *Laborem Exercens*] (Washington DC, 1981).

[34] *DT*, I, p. 342. On this theme as applied to the theology of the eucharist see my article 'Presentation of the Gifts: Orthodox Insights for Western Liturgical Renewal,' *Worship*, 60, no. 1 (1986): 22–38, and Chapter 6 below.

The element of freedom is decisive here if such an attitude is to occur within a life of faith. Stăniloae continues,

> To be sure, every man performs a labour by virtue of powers given to him by God. However, it is within his power not to use his abilities for labour through which he returns the things received with man's stamp upon them, that is, valued by him.[35]

Each person has the power freely to choose whether he will increase the talents he has been given or not. The purpose of such labour, then, is nothing less than the self-disclosure of God to his creation and that of humankind to God:

> In essence, through the gift of the world God desires to make himself known to man in love. Therefore, man must rise above the gifts he has received to God who gave them. The gift, understood as a sign of the love of one person for another, is by its very nature destined to be transcended in favour of the one who has given it. In a way, the gift is the thing which the person who has *given* it renounces out of love for the person *to* whom he gives it.[36]

A New Spirituality

Although the trajectory of the dialogue of the gift is, in the end, transcendent, Godward, it has a horizontal, human dimension as well. Within the context of highly industrialized and technological societies, and especially in totalitarian states, that fashioning of the infinite components of the natural world inevitably assumes a corporate, communal aspect. Now more than ever the fashioning of our priestly gift can become a common endeavour. The natural world, in being so acted upon, can contribute positively toward greater solidarity between people. In this way, contends Stăniloae, our labour becomes a major force in eliciting unity amidst legitimate human diversity. It becomes a means by which we reflect more fully God's own trinitarian life. Moreover, through our united endeavours in refashioning nature we disclose ourselves to one another in new

[35] Ibid.
[36] Ibid.; italics mine.

ways, thus becoming 'transparent subjects' in a more profound communion of love. Labour becomes a sign of love, says Stăniloae, since through its fatiguing, ascetical character it spiritualizes men and women and the fruits that nature gives to them.[37]

Not only can the exercise of this imaginative mastery lead us to deeper communion with one another, but that same communion should provoke each person to an even greater thirst to uncover the limitless alterations possible in the natural order.[38] In summing up the spiritual significance of human labour he concludes:

> Today God unites us more among ourselves and by this solidarity causes us to grow spiritually through labour and sacrifice. *This is a new asceticism*, a positive asceticism, applicable to all and demanded from all. It is one which, though not contrary to the old forms, is able to lend them a new sustaining power. Our God-given responsibility before the natural world appears today as a trust to use its resources with discretion and not to pollute it to the point of adulteration.[39]

All the various aspects of this solidarity or bond between man and the natural world must be seen within the broader eschatological hope of salvation and deification in Jesus Christ.

> The impossibility of separating human persons from cosmic nature means that the salvation and perfection of persons is projected onto the whole of nature, while it simultaneously depends upon nature.[40]

Therefore, says Stăniloae, 'the whole of the natural order is destined for the glory which men will share in the Kingdom of Heaven, just as even now it is responsive to the peace and light that radiates from the holy man.'[41] Every labour of the human mind, imagination or body is, therefore, a decisive moment. It

---

[37] Ibid., p. 326.
[38] Ibid., p. 327.
[39] Ibid., p. 328; italics mine.
[40] Ibid., p. 324.
[41] Ibid., pp. 324–325.

is either a movement on behalf of natural harmony and human solidarity or else one that fosters the abuse of the natural order and the disintegration of human solidarity with God and one another.

As I suggested earlier, Fr. Stăniloae's theological perspective is epitomized by his desire for balance. In the case of his theology of the created world that balance can be seen in his unselfconscious ability to comprehend within his theological scheme perspectives which are often opposed and to do so in a way that is not at the expense of theological consistency and dynamism. For example, he effectively depicts an ordered natural universe within which man is firmly rooted, involved and, to a large degree, shaped. At the same time, Fr. Stăniloae not only preserves man's existential freedom but makes that transcendent freedom the very core of his solidarity within the ordered natural world.

In a similarly balanced way Maximus's theology of the creative *Logos* and the created *logoi* bridges the often opposed theologies of divine transcendence on the one hand, and divine immanence on the other. If the *Logos* in his essence is unknowable, the *logoi* of all created things bespeak a real divine involvement in the world not only in creating, but in sustaining and bringing it to fulfillment in deification. As microcosm humanity can share in that task.

Even more significant, perhaps, is Stăniloae's description of the world as gift. It is one with profoundly rich implications for contemporary spirituality. Including, as it does, a renewed emphasis upon humanity's natural priesthood in the exercise of human labour, it provides a way of integrating much of our modern industrial and technological cultures and societies into the Christian movement Godward. The significance of this for our whole understanding of the scope of salvation in Christ should not be under-valued. It may be that the persistent absence – until recently at least – of a cosmic view of salvation in western theology is as much the consequence of an unbalanced spirituality as of anything else. If Aelred Squire is right when he traces the origins of our own 'unbearably disincarnate' form of Christianity to the Great Schism with the Christian east, then the 'new asceticism' that Fr. Stăniloae commends could prove to be an immensely positive, even radical contribution.[42]

By his understanding of the world as gift of God given back to God by humanity's priestly labour, Stăniloae's *Dogmatic Theology* endeavours to make known the world's positive significance for our growth into God. Such a purpose is at its heart an evangelical one, since such a theology is meant to give humankind the same sense of superiority over technology as the Gospel and patristic theology gave to classical man in the face of nature.[43] Aware that in our generation the science-based industrial and technological system has at times become an overwhelming social force and a hindrance to human freedom, Stăniloae insists upon its potential to further our freedom in Christ. To that end theology

> . . . is called upon to deliver man from the feeling that he is crushed by technology, just as the Gospel and the teaching of the Fathers delivered him from the feeling that he was at the discretion of certain capricious spiritual beings who made use of nature in an arbitrary way.[44]

It is a theology that affirms human sovereignty over nature, science and technology. It reminds us that labour, technology and production exist for man and not vice versa. His theology acknowledges the spiritual centrality of creative human effort, and the gift potential of all things. At the same time it challenges us to transcend the gifts we both receive and give in loving communion with one another and with the Giver of all good things who will, in the end, draw all things back to himself in the final liberation for which the whole creation awaits in hope (Rom. 8.20).

---

[42] Aelred Squire, *Asking the Fathers* (London, 1973), p. 56.
[43] So Stăniloae remarks in *Theology and the Church* ('The Problems and Perspectives of Orthodox Theology,' p. 225).
[44] Ibid.

5

Christ, Creation and the Cross

An accurate appraisal of Fr. Stăniloae's theology of the created order must acknowledge the criticism that his vision is too hopeful.[1] Is it not naively unaware of the struggle and tension, the inadequacy and brokenness which characterizes our human experience? Does it admit the estrangement which the human spirit often suffers through its unavoidable engagement with the world in which we live? With those concerns in mind this chapter seeks to draw out another side of Stăniloae's thought which his theology of creation is rooted in, namely, his soteriological vision of the crucified God.

Those acquainted with the history of Christian theology will recognize the phrase 'theology of the cross' as one with a specific origin and reference in the theological tradition. It was coined by the Augustinian monk Martin Luther in 1518, and around it was gradually woven the whole fabric of Luther's radical new understanding not just of our salvation but of Christian theology as a whole, of God's self-communication and of our knowledge of God.[2] In the hands of Luther and much

---

[1] John Meyendorff records this criticism in his Foreword to Stăniloae, *Theology and the Church*, p. 9.

[2] Alister E. McGrath, *Luther's Theology of the Cross. Martin Luther's Theological Breakthrough* (Oxford, 1985), p. 1.

of the subsequent Protestant tradition that theology of the cross has come to signify a theological vision with its own powerful and distinctive contours: Christocentric, with especial emphasis upon 'the crucified God' (another of Luther's bold phrases); anthropocentric in its view of the object of God's saving activity; and built upon a radical separation between natural and revealed theology, between the order of nature and the order of grace.

None of those characteristics seems agreeable to Orthodox theology as we have come to know it either in its patristic sources or in the writings of its great twentieth-century expositors.[3] So it may seem doubly curious to ascribe to Fr. Stăniloae's thought anything like a *theologia crucis* in its traditional western sense. Given the fact that his *Orthodox Dogmatic Theology* makes only one specific mention of the cross in its section headings we might well conclude that even a highly modified theology of the cross is of little consequence within the overall picture. But that would be a mistake. For in the *Dogmatic Theology* as well as in numerous articles and essays we find an explicit, cogent and integrated discussion of the cross in Christian theology and experience. It is more explicit, more integral to the overall substance of Stăniloae's theology than it is among many contemporary Orthodox writers.

The Cross as an Ecumenical Issue

It might be worth while pausing for a moment to consider why this is so. It is notable, I think, that several of his essays on the significance of the cross appear in the ecumenical section of the Romanian journal *Ortodoxia*, under 'Interconfessional Problems.' There we find, I believe, one of the chief motives for Stăniloae's attention to the theology of the cross: his long-standing engagement with the western Christian tradition, especially those forms with which his own Romanian context has put him in touch, forms which happen to be both Catholic

---

[3] E.g. the writings of Sergei Bulgakov, Vladimir Lossky or Georges Florovsky, to name but a few.

and Protestant.[4] Remember that his native Transylvania has had and still has a diverse religious history where interconfessional exchange, sometimes even confrontation, have been part of Christian life for centuries.

Nor could Stăniloae avoid the Protestant tradition, which was so strong in Transylvania, when he took up theological studies in western Europe. Reference has already been made to his brief period of study in Munich when the neo-orthodoxy of Karl Barth was gaining the ascendancy.[5] Among Protestant theologians that same period, which witnessed the demise of German Liberal Protestantism, saw the revival of the theology of the cross. It may be from that first experience of 'crisis' theology in the West that Stăniloae's interest in the theology of the cross first arose. But whatever its sources or motivations as a theological theme, Fr. Stăniloae has developed a theology of the cross and of the crucified God in such a way as to give it greater prominence than it sometimes has in Orthodox thought, yet in a way that accords with the rather different sensibilities of the Orthodox theological tradition and with his distinctive theological vision. What, then, would it mean to develop a theology of the cross on those terms? In Fr. Stăniloae's case it means seeing the cross integrated into a theology which balances creation and salvation, the order of nature and the order of grace. That, therefore, is the framework in which his theology of the cross is presented here.

The Cross and Creation

It is, in fact, with regard to the doctrine of creation that the cross finds explicit mention in the headings of Stăniloae's *Dogmatic Theology*. That correlation sets Fr. Stăniloae's thinking about the cross in very different terms from the Lutheran tradition out of which the *theologia crucis* first arose. It is well known that in Luther's theology of the cross, and in the theological tradition to which it gave rise, there is an uneasy connection between creation and its relation to God's revelation

---

[4] See Chapter 1, pp. 8–9.
[5] See Chapter 1, p. 14.

in Christ. Luther, for instance, conceded that a natural theology provided useful knowledge about God as a preparation for that knowledge given through revelation. But, he went on to say, once revelation has come the crucified God totally displaces the created order as a locus of our knowledge of God and his saving purpose.[6] That radical separation between nature and grace Stăniloae, in fact, criticized when it was re-expressed by Karl Barth.[7] Stăniloae's theology of the cross, on the other hand, finds its place within a framework in which the sources of revelation are not so limited or self-contained. Again, the opening words of the *Dogmatic Theology* quoted in Chapter 2 should be recalled: 'The Orthodox Church does not separate natural revelation and supernatural. Natural revelation is known and fully understood in light of the supernatural revelation.'[8] Fr. Stăniloae's theology of the cross exemplifies this continuity between natural and supernatural revelation. To appreciate that continuity it is helpful to recall the key points of Fr. Stăniloae's theology of creation.

In keeping with the opening assertion of the *Dogmatic Theology* which has already been quoted, the world is intended as the first point of divine-human communication: 'the first act of God towards the world, which can be considered as the basis of all his further acts and of God's continuing revelation, is the creation.'[9] Stăniloae speaks of an intimate 'solidarity' between humanity and the world in relation to God. So, far from being a neutral context of our life and spiritual growth, the created world in fact has no meaning apart from our existence. So inter-dependent are they that the world can be said to exist 'for spiritual formation in the vision of the life to come.'[10]

[6] McGrath, *Cross*, pp. 162–163.

[7] Stăniloae seeks to balance Karl Barth's stress on the separation between God and man with the doctrine of the divine energies – the divine power/action by which the transcendent God actually connects with, speaks to, and meets us – associated with the Byzantine theologian St. Gregory Palamas (Beauregard, p. 22).

[8] *DT*, I, p. 9.

[9] *Theology and the Church* ('Revelation Through Acts, Words and Images'), p. 113.

[10] *DT*, I, p. 340.

Stăniloae develops this understanding of the created order through his distinctive theme of the world as gift. As has already been noted, to speak of a gift is to speak not so much of a thing but of a process of personal interaction which is expressed in Stăniloae's phrase, the 'dialogue of the gift.'[11] 'When we receive a gift from somebody,' he explains, 'we should look primarily towards the person who has given it and not keep our eyes fixed on the gift.'[12]

But the dialogue of the gift requires more than an acknowledgement of the gift. He goes on: it should elicit an acknowledgement of the giver. When properly given and received, a gift points beyond itself; it becomes the occasion of a personal communication and self-disclosure, an occasion of self-disclosure. The 'dialogue of the gift' is really what Stăniloae calls a 'dialogue of love.'[13] The very meaning and purpose of the gift is that it be continually transcended in a communion of love. That truth at the level of personal human interaction is by analogy descriptive of the relationship between God and humanity, that is, between the 'supreme and eternal Person,' on the one hand, and human persons on the other.

On this all-embracing scale the world is given by God the creator as a gift. As the fundamental medium for the dialogue of the gift, the created order, including human existence itself, is meant to be the means of dialogue and communion between God and us. Stăniloae insists: 'When God created all things that he might share his love, the purpose of all things was that they might attain to full participation in this love, that is, to full communion with God.'[14] God has created the world to be that context. As a symbol of this purpose Stăniloae looks to the wood of the tree in Paradise created to be 'transparent' and 'open' to what he calls 'an infinite and paradisal depth.'[15] That depth is nothing other than the infinite being of God. The world and its life, then, are given by God as a gift, that is, as the means

[11] Ibid., p. 341. See above pp. 58–60.
[12] *Victory*, p. 5.
[13] *DT*, I, p. 340.
[14] Ibid., p. 338.
[15] 'The Cross in Orthodox Theology and Worship,' *Sobernost*, series 7, no. 4 (1977): 236.

whereby we, receiving and giving back in return, are drawn to look upon the Giver and so enjoy personal communication and communion with God. As the previous chapter pointed out, in such a dialogue we are not meant to be passive. As men and women who are given a priestly dominion over the Lord's creation, we are called to a reciprocal act of gift-giving. We are to use and experience creation, indeed life itself, so as to make it a perpetual gift-offering back to God. That response of humanity constitutes our natural priesthood. As priest, humanity is called to acknowledge the world as gift, and is called to present it back to God. This priestly offering is to become the means of communion and fellowship with God.

The Gift and the Cross

Such an understanding of the creation as gift is for Stăniloae inextricably connected with the cross. The world, as has been said, is a gift from God whose purpose is to unite humanity to God. It is meant, therefore, to display the essential dynamic of every gift, namely, that it be transcended. But the dialogue of the gift, in its true and authentic form, as an experience of reciprocity, no longer occurs. For his part God continues to speak, to give his gifts, not least because he continually sustains the world in being. However, we, for our part, fail to respond. The Fall has disrupted the genuine dialogue of the gift. In Adam humanity lost its power for a true vision of the world. The world's original transparency has become obscured for Adam and Eve and their descendants. In fact, says Stăniloae, the created order itself has even acquired a mastery over humanity by drawing humankind's gaze upon 'sensible nature' alone.[16] The consequence of this is that we fail to experience the world as a means of ever deepening personal communion with God, the Giver of the gift of the world. Whereas it was given to be transparent to God for us, it has now become opaque. Though God continues to give it as his gift to us, as a word to us, still full of potential offerings for dialogue and communion, we have become so attached to the gift itself that we have forgotten

[16] Ibid.

who has given it to us.[17] We do not experience it as gift because we do not recognize the Giver from whom it comes. We all know how this happens even in our common everyday experience. In receiving a gift we all have the tendency to become fascinated or indeed obsessed by the gift itself to the neglect or exclusion of communion between giver and receiver which the gift is meant to foster. In other words, through Adam we prefer a condition of self-centred possession to the self-giving of inter-personal communion, to the self-transcendence implied in true response to God the Giver. In so doing, we have ceased to be responsible partners in the relationship of dialogue with God, and we no longer acknowledge that God is seeking to communicate with us.[18] Such, then, is the circumstance of the world, and humanity, created but now fallen.

The Cross and Salvation

With all this as the background we find that Stăniloae develops a theology of the cross and a doctrine of salvation which wholly builds upon rather than rejects the natural order as a real component in our saving knowledge of God in Christ and in our experience of God's saving acts in Christ and the Holy Spirit. Because of the solidarity between humankind and creation in our spiritual growth, salvation cannot be construed in the way the traditional theology of the cross does, that is, as something wholly extrinsic to human nature. Rather, it must be such as to restore to that nature the power of its destined priesthood through which the dialogue of love is engaged. Within such an approach the agenda on behalf of us and our salvation is to re-establish the dialogue of love between God and humankind. How is this to happen?

It is interesting that for Stăniloae even the cross of Christ itself is not viewed as something essentially distinct from humankind and its experience of the natural world. We hear echoes of the discussion of natural and supernatural revelation in Chapter 1. The shadow of the cross hangs back, so to speak, over the fallen

---

[17] *Victory*, p. 5.
[18] Ibid., p. 10.

world and human experience because, in our fallenness, we ascribe to our world and our experiences an ultimacy which they inevitably do not possess. Drawing again upon Maximus the Confessor, Stăniloae speaks of a kind of cross etched into the fabric of the world since the Fall. All things anticipate the crucifixion; all things manifest a brokenness when their claim to ultimacy is discredited either by destruction, by pain or by death.[19]

Fallen humanity, set within a fallen world, inevitably involves a despair akin to what Luther described as *Anfechtung*. For Luther *Anfechtung* signified a condition of hopelessness and helplessness bred of man's conflict with the world and with his mortality. That experience is part of his Law-Gospel dialectic in which our inevitable frustration and failure in living the Law impels us to the foot of the cross where God's unmerited word of forgiveness can be heard. The experience of *Anfechtung*, Luther insisted, has its source in God who, by that means draws us to his mercy.[20] In contrast to Luther, Stăniloae emphasizes the natural experience of the cross. This natural experience of the cross, because it is only natural, leads nowhere; it has no vista beyond itself; it is spiritually opaque, existentially blinding. In other words, for Stăniloae there is an *Anfechtung* intrinsic to the fallen human condition. But that only goes part of the way in explaining this *Anfechtung* in Stăniloae's theology of the cross.

Because such an experience of the world can often be denied and to some extent avoided, in the end it is God's task in saving to transform this pattern and experience. That, argues Stăniloae, can be done only by revealing that the world, and all aspects of creativity are a gift and as such point to our destiny in dialogue and communion with God the Giver. When humankind is

---

[19] Ibid., p. 6.

[20] The word comes from the religious experience of Luther and epitomizes that condition in which man is acutely aware of his need for the Gospel. 'It is all the doubt, turmoil, pang, tremor, panic, despair, desolation and desperation which invade the spirit of man.' So Roland Bainton, in his biography of Luther, *Here I Stand* (Tring, 1978) p. 42. See the remarks of Alister McGrath which put the notion in the context of Luther's theology of the cross, *Cross*, pp. 169–175; esp. pp. 170–171.

mesmerized by the gift to the neglect of the Giver, the gift, says Stăniloae, must somehow be broken and its insufficiency as a means of personal fulfillment revealed. In our fallen condition, therefore, every gift, even the gift of life itself, 'requires a certain cross, and this cross is meant to show us that all these gifts are not the last and final reality.'[21]

Thus dialogue, the dialogue of love, and woundedness, brokenness and sacrifice are joined in the restoration of human-kind and the world. So, Jesus's role as prophet and teacher is of a piece with his role as sacrificial victim. Jesus, as the Word of God, as agent of dialogue and communion between us and God, must also be crucified man. Amid a fallen world dialogue returns only through sacrifice. Jesus cannot be thought of as Christ and as saviour, therefore, apart from the cross.[22]

What happened on the cross? For Stăniloae the Old Testament figure of Job is a type of Christ crucified, and as such provides insight into the meaning of the crucifixion. Job exemplifies both the fallen human condition and the nature of God's loving and saving response. Job's burdens, his sufferings, his deprivations, are all designed to draw his attention away from the gifts God gives, even the gift of life, to the Giver himself. 'God in effect says to Job,' Fr. Stăniloae explains, 'All my gifts are wonderful, but the intention of their wonder is to reveal the infinite wisdom and greatness of the one who gives them all.' Job's declaration, '. . . now mine eye seeth thee,' at the end of all his trials (42.1–3, 5–6), explains Stăniloae, 'means to say that up until this moment Job had always thought of God in much the same terms in which others had spoken of him; now he begins to understand God himself, beyond all his gifts, the Giver of everything . . . He saw God in a higher way than is possible merely through his gifts. He saw him immediately through his suffering.'[23]

That is the process which is at work finally and perfectly in Jesus Christ. His death on the cross reveals the partialness, the incompleteness, the woundedness of any created being or

---

[21] *Victory*, p. 5.
[22] 'Cross,' pp. 238–239.
[23] *Victory*, p. 17.

relationship. And yet, amidst it all, even at the moment of utmost dereliction, when the gift of life itself is to be taken away, Jesus looks beyond to the Giver of the gift; he loves the Giver even when all the gifts have been taken away. In Jesus, most concentratedly on the cross, the dialogue of love between God and humankind is perfect, wholly unobstructed by distraction from the gifts themselves, even the gift of life at the point of its imminent loss. Thus, the wood of the tree of Paradise becomes transparent again insofar as Christ, the new Adam, uses that wood to see beyond into the infinite love and being of God. 'The cross,' he writes, 'with its two lines, one vertical, the other horizontal, produces a wound in the total reality of creation; and through the wound God, who is at once beyond creation yet pierces through into its midst, is made visible.'[24] *'Deus absconditus sed revelatus.'* In revealing the brokenness of the gift of the world the crucified Christ draws our gaze beyond to the Giver.

So for Stăniloae, as for Luther, the crucifixion is the revelatory moment. Whereas for Luther it hinges on the response of faith by which our sin becomes Christ's righteousness, for Stăniloae it is the event by means of which humankind, reduced to a remnant in Christ himself, is empowered by God to cleave to the Giver above the gift. The cross of Christ epitomizes our renewed potential to encounter the Giver through his gifts in an ever-deepening momentum of exchange. It is the supreme moment when the dialogue of love again prevails.

The cross, therefore, signifies for Stăniloae a God who, as infinite Person, is above all his gifts. At the same time it expresses a perfect relationship between God, humankind's creator, and created existence itself, since in Christ the relationship between the divine Giver, the gift and the human receiver has been perfectly realized.[25] Stăniloae describes the effect of Christ's crucifixion in re-establishing the dialogue like this:

---

[24] 'The Holy Cross as the Centre of Holiness and Blessing, and Focus of Reverence,' *Ortodoxia*, 34, no. 1 (1975), no page. Translation my own.
[25] *Victory*, p. 20.

Without the cross man would be in danger of considering this world as the ultimate reality. Without the cross he would no longer see the world as God's gift. Without the cross the Son of God incarnate would have simply confirmed the image of the world as it is now as the final reality, and strictly speaking he could have been neither God nor God incarnate. The cross completes the fragmentary meaning of this world which has meaning when it is seen as a gift which has its value, but only a relative and not an absolute value.[26]

In wounding the world, the crucified Lord illuminates the world. The cross perfects the creation as cosmos.

The restoration of the world as gift depends upon the restoration of humanity's freedom as described in the first chapters of Genesis. The Fall, according to Stăniloae, signals the loss of humanity's sovereignty over nature, its freedom in relation to nature. In the eating of the fruit, sensible nature acquired dominance over the human spirit, and men and women became enslaved to their bodily tendencies, tendencies which are more at home with an opaque nature than with a nature transparent to God. So, humanity's return to that freedom of spirit and priestly offering for which it was created depends upon an inner strengthening by Christ.[27] For Stăniloae the cross is, as the patristic tradition teaches, the pre-eminent battle between good and evil because there the human spirit and will are energized to their fullest potential by the divine life and power. That empowering is nothing less than the desire for God above all his gifts, desiring God at all costs, even the cost of self. The cross, then, is the concentrated expression of that spiritual power of the God-man, whereby the true self, as autonomous reality, is broken and laid aside and the self, as person in communion with God and with others through creation, rises. Because it expresses this triumph of the free human spirit, says Stăniloae, the cross 'teaches us to live in relation to God and nature, and gives us the power to do it, not as those who abandon themselves to the impersonal impulses of nature, but those who, in communion with God, strengthen

26 Ibid.
27 'Cross,' p. 237.

their spirit, go beyond themselves and by a death-resurrection transform nature into an offering.'[28]

The Cross and the Spirit of Resurrection

In a perspective such as this, Stăniloae insists, the cross and the resurrection form 'an indissoluble union.'[29] He is critical of any tendency to separate the events as if, for instance, the cross issued from the manward side and the resurrection from the Godward. The cross can only be what it is in Stăniloae's scheme if it is enacted by the God-man. Likewise the resurrection. The two events are not two acts; rather, they are two stages of expression of a single act of divine power. The resurrection event contains and expresses the power of Christ unleashed at the crucifixion; that same power exercised on the cross is then made available, 'perpetuated,' to use Stăniloae's word, in the resurrection. The resurrection, in fact, is the full manifestation of the power which Christ exercised in his voluntary passion on the cross.[30] The resurrection expresses the glorious truth hidden in the scandal of the cross: that in Christ the world, human life and experience, even death itself, become once again transparent to God. The cross's power 'is extended and remains always present in the resurrection, and so also in the risen Christ until the end of the ages.'[31]

Elsewhere Stăniloae speaks of an 'actualizing' of the energy which Christ showed at his crucifixion. There is the point of contact between Stăniloae's theology of the cross and his doctrine of the Spirit. The cross, says Stăniloae, has a 'pneumatic' power and the resurrection is the manifestation and extension of that same power.[32] The experience of the cross becomes the means whereby the uncreated energies are poured forth by the Spirit upon creation. For the Spirit, as the Spirit of communion, is the very power whereby Christ vanquished

---

[28] Ibid.
[29] Ibid., p. 236.
[30] Ibid., p. 234.
[31] Ibid.
[32] Ibid., p. 241.

possessiveness and all forms of humanity's claims to exist by
and for itself or for this world alone.[33] Through their solidarity
with the resurrection power of the crucified God believers too
can be opened to the Giver who is beyond, to 'the radiance
shining from a transcendent person whose object in revealing
himself is to raise us up to him.'[34] Christ's self-emptying on the
cross, his *kenosis*, becomes the means of the pouring forth of the
Spirit who then gradually elevates humankind and creation
toward the divine life.

A Theology of Hope

Stăniloae's *theologia crucis* is notable in that it is interwoven with
his theology of creation, and the link is his theme of the created
world as gift. In keeping with his assertion of the continuity
between God's act of revelation in creation and salvation, the
fallen created world experiences the cross; but it experiences it
as a saving cross only through the mutual work of Christ and
the Spirit. The former makes of that cross in human experience
a vehicle for a dialogue of love with God; the latter makes
Christ's experience our own by continuing the dialogic power
of the cross and the resurrection through history.

Stăniloae places humanity and its natural priesthood at the
centre of his theology of gift, and at the centre of his understanding of salvation. Nevertheless, the theology of the world
as gift means that humanity's salvation cannot occur apart from
the created order. His, therefore, cannot be an anthropocentric
doctrine of salvation. Nature, man and God (to use William
Temple's phrase) are joined in more than a notional way in
Stăniloae's theology of the cross. That too is consonant with
the continuity between creation and salvation which he affirms.

Equally, the crucified God himself cannot for Stăniloae be
regarded as such unless he is seen to be the one 'by whom all
things were made.' The battle and victory on the cross is the
battle and victory of the *Logos*, the Word, who through his
crucifixion renewed for the world its potential as a dialogic

---

[33] Ibid.
[34] *Holiness*, p. 12. Such is Fr. Stăniloae's definition of holiness.

word or conversation between God and humankind. The cross re-creates a freedom for dialogue; through its power, expressed in the resurrection, the dialogue of love is nurtured in expectation of communion in the life of the triune God.

In his influential study, *The Crucified God*, Jürgen Moltmann has written: 'Today the church and theology must turn to the crucified Christ in order to show the world the freedom he offers. This is essential if they wish to become what they assert they are: the church of Christ, and Christian theology.'[35] Moltmann's words arise from the struggles and tragedies of western Europe in our century, and they seek to re-capture the theology of Luther in its most startling, radical form. Stăniloae's theology of the cross, different in so many ways from the tradition out of which Moltmann speaks, is a theological vision of equal power and equal hope. Without minimizing the radical fact of the crucified God, Stăniloae links his theology of the cross to the created world in which we live, to the lesser crosses which every human person inevitably bears. He thereby offers an intelligible, hopeful point of contact between the heart of the Christian mystery and the woundedness of human experience. Such an approach may, as I have hinted, have ecumenical significance. It surely has a real pastoral, evangelistic and apologetic value as Christians try to draw the world back into dialogue with its creator, whose Word first brought it into being and still sustains it in love.

[35] *The Crucified God* (London, 1974), p. 1.

6

Creation, Sacrament and Church

The theological score composed so far looks toward a resolution. In particular, the theme of creation as gift and of humanity's priestly role, coupled with Stăniloae's presentation of Christ and creation in the economy of salvation, need to be brought together. The reference at the end of the previous chapter to the 'actualizing' of the energy of the crucified Christ by the Spirit of resurrection brings us to this point. Here, as in the *Orthodox Dogmatic Theology* itself, the movement of thought leads to a consideration of the sacraments, particularly the eucharist. As well as being a fitting conclusion to the themes explored in the preceding chapters, Stăniloae's eucharistic theology provides a fascinating angle on the relationship between liturgy and creation which has become a concern in western liturgical theology in recent years. Both Orthodox and western Christians may therefore find Stăniloae's views provocative and helpful as they seek to enter that particular dialogue.[1]

Sacrament or Mystery?

The spiritual sensibility of Orthodoxy is pre-eminently a sacramental one. As its expositors and apologists have often

---

[1] See, for instance, the wide-ranging *festschrift* entitled *Creation and Liturgy*, ed. Ralph N. McMichael, Jr. (Washington DC, 1993).

claimed, Orthodoxy sees in the created order a rich sacramental potential.[2] Little wonder, then, that in contrast to western Christianity's numerically fixed sacramental 'system,' the Orthodox tradition has found it difficult to restrict the sacraments to a set quantity. Through the centuries the 'sacraments' have been as few as two and as many as ten.[3] Stăniloae has inherited that sensibility. Indeed, its implied sense of the natural order as means of God's communication and action accords with the link, suggested by the Romanian language itself, between the world and the light of manifestation.[4]

When Stăniloae turns to the sacraments in the third volume of the *Dogmatic Theology* the tapestry of themes developed in earlier volumes appears in a succinct yet synthetic way. At a glance the discussion seems conventional enough; Stăniloae even conforms to the seven-fold enumeration of the sacraments common among Roman Catholics and many Anglicans. Quickly, however, we find ourselves in a different and distinctive world.

In the *Dogmatic Theology*, as in other writings, Stăniloae uses the Romanian word *taina* (from the Slavonic тайна) instead of the word *sacrament* (also a Romanian word) commonly used in the West. *Taina* is the Romanian rendering of the Greek *'mysterion,'* or 'mystery,' by which the Orthodox signify 'sacrament.' His use of the word 'mystery', as in the 'holy mysteries', then, is in keeping with general Orthodox usage when speaking of the sacraments of the church. But there is more to it. As we have seen in other areas of his thought, so in his sacramental theology the influence of Maximus the Confessor is strong. Stăniloae imbues the word *taina,* or 'mystery,' with a strong maximian flavour.

Maximus's own sense of *mysterion* is dense indeed and cannot readily be tied to one consistent definition or usage.[5] If there is a common signification, however, it seems to be God's

[2] So Philip Sherrard in his essay 'The Sacrament', in *The Orthodox Ethos. Studies in Orthodoxy*, ed. A. J. Phillippou (Oxford, 1964), pp. 133–139.

[3] Ware, *Orthodox Church*, pp. 281–283.

[4] See above, p. 27.

[5] Thunberg, *Man*, p. 164.

movement toward union with and in the creation. Therefore *mysterion*, or *taina*, can refer widely to God's primordial act of creation; more particularly, to his act of incarnation; and, more specifically still, to the sacramental life of the church. Perhaps Maximus's sense of 'mystery' is most succinctly expressed in a statement from the *Ambigua*: 'God the Word of God wills always and in all things to work the mystery of entering into the body of what has been created.'[6] In light of that understanding Stăniloae can speak of the comprehensive mystery which embraces the world and humankind together. 'The whole of existence is a mystery', he maintains. 'The cosmos is a mystery; the world around us is a mystery; my own person is a mystery and my fellow human beings are a mystery.'[7] Here we see a clear appropriation of Maximus's usage. For Stăniloae it means nothing less than the 'active presence' of the 'absolutely Transcendent' amidst the world and humankind.[8]

With that basic sense of mystery in mind we can better appreciate Stăniloae's own exposition of the mysteries or sacraments and, in particular, the eucharist, the chief sacramental mystery. Indeed, it is possible already to see how his discussion links the Christian sacramental life to some of themes described in earlier chapters. In addition, it brings ecclesiology into the scope of these considerations in an explicit way. Not that a precise doctrine of the church is presented here; rather, the essential line which connects church with the eucharist, creation and the priestly character of humanity is highlighted.

Humanity and Creation: the 'First Mystery'

Because of the highly integrated character of Stăniloae's thought there are numerous points of entry into the subject at hand. In keeping with his creation-affirming approach, however, Stăniloae introduces his general discussion of the

---

[6] *PG*, 91:1084D; Stăniloae refers to this text, *DT*, III, p. 9, note 1.

[7] 'The Mystery of the Church,' in *Church, Kingdom, World. The Church as Mystery and Prophetic Sign*, ed. Gennadios Limouris (Geneva, 1986), p. 50.

[8] Ibid., p. 51. Commentators on Stăniloae's view of 'mystery' have not always shown an appreciation for the influence of Maximus's thought; for instance, Charles Hill, *Mystery of Life. A Theology of Church* (Dublin, 1991), p. 4.

sacraments in the *Dogmatic Theology* by considering the 'created component' of the sacraments. But there is no rush to consider the 'matter' of the sacraments (e.g. bread, wine, water) in the way a traditional sacramental theology might. Instead, Stăniloae articulates the fundamental components not of the sacraments *per se*, viewed as objects, but of sacramental action in general. 'At the foundation of the Orthodox Church's concept of the mysteries,' he says,

> is belief in the power of the divine Spirit of Christ [working] from within one human being toward another, through the means of their bodies and the matter [or materials] which they share between them, in the context of the Church, the mystical body of Christ.[9]

We must note first the succession of themes in this definition: Spirit, humanity, the material creation, and the church. His sacramental theology takes shape from a finely developed understanding of the interrelation of those elements. A striking aspect of this initial definition of the sacraments is its emphasis on human persons, the sacramental actors. We might expect such an emphasis in a discussion of, say, marriage or ordination. But Stăniloae sees the human person, more precisely one human person interacting with another, as the first definitive feature of a sacrament.

Why this emphasis on the personal agent of the sacrament? We can recognize even in this preliminary statement aspects of anthropology derived from Maximus which we have touched upon in earlier chapters. In fact, in the first few pages of the *Dogmatic Theology*'s discussion of the sacraments Stăniloae invokes Maximus's view of humanity as the 'link' (*sýndesmos*) within the created order.[10] As we saw before, that role arises from humanity's dual composition as spirit and body. His spiritual side expresses itself in the capacity to think, to will and to love; his bodily side in tangible involvement with the created world in which he lives and through which he expresses the capacities especially linked to

[9] *DT*, III, p. 7.
[10] Ibid., pp. 10–11.

his spiritual nature.[11] Although there is tension between the manifold expressions of those two dimensions of his existence, humanity's microcosmic role seeks to steer them toward fruitful interaction. By this unitive role, says Stăniloae, humankind 'is to become the conscious and voluntary means by which God fulfils and completes' his union with the creation.[12] In this way humanity takes a principal part in expressing the unity between the *Logos* by whom all things were made and the creation which is his work.[13]

This is the heart of what may be called Stăniloae's sacramental anthropology. That is, in humankind, viewed as microcosm and mediator, there exists the fundamental dynamic inherent in the sacraments: the bonding of matter and spirit to express the unitive purpose of the *Logos*. But Stăniloae's initial description also points to the presence of the Holy Spirit. As his discussion develops it is clear that his sacramental anthropology, with its stress upon the personal foundation of sacramental action, relies upon the fact that the human person, in his or her spiritual dimension, is apt to become a vehicle for the Holy Spirit to act. This allows for an effectual link between the Holy Spirit and the material world through the embodied human spirit. That spirit is in touch with the Holy Spirit through its rational and volitional powers in so far as they are energized by faith. It is also in touch with the material creation as embodied or incarnate spirit. Therefore, as a corollary to that foundational concept described above, Stăniloae affirms that 'the divine Spirit is able to work through the medium of the human spirit upon the matter [material] of the cosmos generally as well as upon other persons.'[14]

But as we have seen in earlier chapters, Stăniloae always keeps in view the horizontal dimension of humankind's bond with creation. Solidarity with creation is never to foster solipsistic or individualistic experience, even if it be a Godward one. That bond exists as a force for unity, the unity of the *Logos*,

[11] Ibid., p. 7.
[12] Ibid., p. 9.
[13] Ibid., pp. 7–8.
[14] Ibid., pp. 7–8.

and so it should contribute toward reciprocity and solidarity between persons. That too, therefore, is an element of sacramental action. It is never the action of one person upon or with the creation even when that person directs the action Godward. It is always an action *between* persons. 'Neither the material, nor the words spoken, nor the gestures performed, taken by themselves, constitute the mystery,' says Stăniloae. Rather, 'the mystery is accomplished in the *coming together* of two human subjects who through faith are open to the Holy Spirit in the context of the church.' And again, 'it is constituted in the meeting in faith of those two persons in the context of the Spirit-filled Church, and in the bodily contact of those two persons.'[15]

This is not subjectivism, however. There can be no sacrament, no mystery, apart from persons' enSpirited engagement with the material world. Here we should recall what Stăniloae has said about the world as gift, as the context of spiritual growth, and about humankind's call to use the gift in rapport with one another and with God. As we shall see below, the sacramental action is nothing less than the actualization of the natural priesthood. Within that framework of the world's purpose as gift, this coming together of persons with the material of the natural world passing between them finds its place. Humanity and the world are by their very createdness and God-given purpose oriented toward mystery or sacramentality, toward a joint Godward movement and influence. Together they form the sphere in which 'God the Word of God wills always and in all things to work the mystery of entering into the body of what has been created.'[16] Maximus's word is *ensomatōsis*, which means 'embodiment' or 'embodying', though it is often translated as 'incarnation.' Whereas the translation 'incarnation' points unequivocally to the 'taking flesh' of the Word of God, the actual word 'embodying' is more general in its reference, not least because it can refer to every created thing. The latter translation may be less attractive but it seems to me to convey Maximus's meaning and Stăniloae's reference more clearly.

---

[15] Ibid., p. 8; italics mine. The Romanian *întîlnire*, translated here as 'coming together' has the complementary sense of 'encounter.'

[16] See note 6 above.

As a microcosm, then, humankind stands at the centre of the mystery of creation. Stăniloae, influenced by Maximus, calls it the 'first and all-encompassing mystery.'[17] It is so called because the energies and works of the 'supreme Mystery,' God, operate within the world which he has created. The 'first mystery' of all created things, in which humanity holds so distinctive a position, signals that all things within it share the quality of mystery or sacrament. Only the human person, however, is aware of this inherent mysterious character; only the human person can actualize the import of this mysterious character for him or herself, for others, or for the material creation. When Stăniloae asserts that all of existence is a mystery, he adds:

> Each of the world's component parts which exists in this relationship with the Transcendent, exists in the general mystery of the world or forms part of the world's mystery as a whole. But only the human person is conscious of this mystery at the heart of the world and of itself as constituting a part of it, being itself a greater mystery than the world. It could be said that the mystery of the world's relationship with the transcendent is powerfully realized in the human person. For in the understanding and experience of the mystery, the human person has an especial capacity for relationship with the Transcendent.[18]

This vision of the primordial intention of God to bring about union with his creation has an eschatological thrust. With Paul's expectation that in the end God 'will be all in all' (1 Cor. 15.28) Stăniloae sees this union between God and the created order, begun in the first act of creation, growing both wider and closer. That perspective, coupled with the key role of humankind in this union of God with creation, fixes the groundwork for Stăniloae's discussion of the relationship between Christ and the sacraments.

Jesus Christ: the 'New Mystery'

Within such a vision of the relationship between creation, man and God, Christology arises as a complementary and

---

[17] Ibid., p. 9.
[18] 'Mystery,' p. 51.

completing feature. Stăniloae does not minimize the Incarnation; however, the highly developed sense of the incarnate Word as the *creative* Word leads him to stress continuity within a divine economy conceived as a whole.

That the incarnate Word is embodied in the fullness of humanity is central to Stăniloae's vision of salvation. In this he is faithful to the essential affirmation of Chalcedonian Christology. The significance of the human form of this embodying or incarnation is this: the fundamental co-operation of man with God *via* the created order is perfectly expressed by and in Jesus Christ. Stăniloae's whole approach to Christology is guided by this heightened co-ordination between creation and anthropology. Unlike so much modern Christology, which has found it difficult to speak meaningfully of God becoming human because it has worked with an underdeveloped doctrine of creation, Stăniloae presents Christology as a coherent, we might even say natural, development of the theme of mystery as it applies to God, then to creation, and only then to humankind.

In this respect the God-Man is a uniquely concentrated expression and fulfillment of humanity's link role by which God and creation, Spirit and matter, incorporeal and corporeal, are joined.[19] That link, already existing in humankind, but limited in action and orientation because of the Fall, is strengthened and perfected in the humanity assumed by the Word. The intrinsically sacramental humanity which he assumed becomes a 'new' and 'climactic mystery' or sacrament. Through complete union with God the Word, the complementary interaction of Spirit and creation, the uncreated and the created, acting through the human spirit, takes place. This incarnation of the Word is not, therefore, a spiritual act in the sense that it does not involve the materiality of Jesus nor the materiality of his human context. Such an incarnation would be no true incarnation because it would not take account of the bond between the uncreated and the created or between humanity and its created milieu. The assumption of the complete psychosomatic complexity of a human being by the Word

---

[19] *DT*, III, p. 11.

occurs so that the same creative Word might unite himself more intimately with all human subjects. As a wholly inSpirited human being, therefore, the God-Man has actualized all undeveloped human potentials so as to become a new, effectual and conscious bond between God and creation. As the unifying power within the creation the *Logos*, or Word, by becoming man, has 'actualized' humanity's unifying powers as microcosm and link. In so doing the Word has not only furthered his creative purpose but he has set within the created order a source of unitive power so that humankind as a whole might share in the movement toward God's full unity with all things.

It is important to see the order of this unifying action of the Word of God. First, it is a union with humanity; an entrance into that unique microcosmic world of persons who are the agents of union between Spirit and matter. Through personal action, that same microcosmic humanity of the Word touches and affects the wider created order. Second, that unifying action extends outward in solidarity with more and more men and women who by faith become members of the Body of Christ. 'Christ,' Stăniloae says, 'is the climactic central mystery from which a power of attraction operates permanently to draw human beings into union with him.'[20]

That this new mystery of Christ might restore and enliven the primordial mystery of creation is, according to Stăniloae, the purpose of the Incarnation. In order that God's creative purpose might come to fulfillment and that the mystery of God's union with his creation might be complete, he

> made the supreme mystery of his active presence a reality in the created world by uniting created humanity with his Son in an inseparable manner . . . By his human nature, which he united with his person, the Son of God ceaselessly remains among us human beings as an active presence, and is thus able all the more easily to communicate his divine perfections to us.[21]

At this point, then, we find the basis upon which a sacramental theology can take shape. Stăniloae has established

---

[20] 'Mystery,' p. 53.
[21] Ibid., p. 52.

the intrinsic bond between humanity and the created order and has asserted the Spirit-bearing potential of nature in conjunction with the human person acting in faith. Finally, he has placed the creative Word of God, Christ crucified and risen, at the centre of the renewal of this mystery of humankind and creation.

The Eucharist

In Stăniloae's exposition of the eucharist the themes developed in this and previous chapters come to bear. This discussion cannot cover the wide range of issues which relate to the eucharist. It can, however, try to show how the eucharist complements key themes which this and previous chapters have explored. In particular, it offers an opportunity to return to the themes of the dialogue of the gift and of the priestly call of humankind.

Determined as he is to maintain a balance between God's transcendence and immanence, Stăniloae describes the unknowable source of Godhead, God the Father, as the 'creative gift-Giving subject.' As such, God is always beyond and 'infinitely superior' to the creation and all created subjects.[22] In contrast, Christ is described as 'the supreme gift of God's love,' a gift 'linked to our nature.'[23] As the Word of God who has assumed creatureliness, Jesus Christ expresses, indeed embodies, creation's full return to the status of gift. Through assumption into the personal being of the Word creation is wholly transparent to God. God is present to and through it in the highest degree possible for created being. The creation becomes the means of encounter between the divine subject and human subjects. The previous chapter examined the meaning of the cross in light of the need to restore to creation and human experience its character as gift. Through his crucifixion Jesus re-invested his humanity with its gift-giving power, and through the resurrection that power opens out into all subsequent history. The eucharist is the flash-point where

[22] *DT*, III, p. 10.
[23] Ibid., p. 12.

Christ the Gift draws us into the dialogue of the gift and restores to both creation and human experience its transparence as gift of God and means of his presence to us and our presence to him.

So far we have followed the line of thought in the *Dogmatic Theology*. However, in an essay Stăniloae sought to explain more extensively than he does in the *Dogmatic Theology* the relationship between the creation, understood as gift, and the mysteries or sacraments of the church.[24] The issue which Stăniloae addresses is one which may have struck the reader already: in what relation does the creation, viewed as mystery and gift in a wide sense, stand with regard to the mysteries of the church properly speaking? Further, how is Stăniloae's hopeful vision of the creation made actual? An earlier chapter described that hopeful vision of the world as gift and means of rapport between God and humankind; another described the opaqueness of the world as we experience it, humanity's sinful inability to see God through his gift or to respond in the dialogue of love. Christ's crucifixion and resurrection were then seen as God's way of restoring to humankind and to the cosmos as a whole its character as gift. That restoration is then actualized through the sacramental life of the church. But why should this be so? Stăniloae asks: 'Does not the consideration of creation itself as the vehicle of God's love and power or as sacrament in the wide sense of the word imply the possibility of our dispensing with the holy mysteries?'[25]

Growing into the Mystery of Christ

The key to Stăniloae's response to the question lies, as the previous discussion has hinted, in the restoration of humankind's ontological and existential bond with Christ, the living gift of God. It is important to emphasize that, following the pattern of the Incarnation of the Word of God himself, it is a

[24] 'Creaţia ca Dar şi Tainele Bisericii' [The Creation as Gift and the Mysteries of the Church] *Ortodoxia*, 28, no. 1 (January–March, 1976): 10–29. Translation my own.
[25] Ibid., 1.

bond *with* Christ *through* creation. Christian sacramental life rises out of belief that we can only experience God *through* his creation, that is, through the experience of it as gift. Any growth into such a realization and such an experience must come through a living and transforming participation in the incarnate Word of God who has made this experience real in himself and possible for others. Stăniloae explains:

> The power to see God's love through the creation and the power to abide in it, and so to remain in the bond of love with God, has been re-established in and through Christ. In this sense there is no separation between Christ and the creation; rather, Christ makes known again and again the character of the creation as gift; he does so by way of a new transformation. He shows in a more accentuated and clear way the love of God manifested through creation, as a sign of God's love. In this sense nature (with human persons as components of the creation) is framed within the order of grace, given that grace, as God's love and power radiating forth through Christ who has assumed the creation in himself, is in fact a clear and more accentuated expression of God's love and power; grace reveals anew the creation as the *milieu* for the manifestation of this love.[26]

The church's sacraments, and here Stăniloae refers chiefly to the eucharist, are the means by which the created order expresses its potential as transparent gift of God rediscovered through union with Christ. Through its assumption by the personal Word of God it is united with the transfigured humanity of Christ and becomes, like that transfigured humanity, a perfect created mode of the dialogue of love.

A Hierarchy of Gifts

The eucharistic gifts of bread and wine which become the sacramental gift of Christ himself do so in a creation-affirming not in a creation-denying way. Their status as mysterious sacramental gifts is, Stăniloae insists, the fulfillment of their status as gift at other levels. Indeed, the creation exists as gift at

[26] Ibid., 2.

different levels or degrees and a rigid distinction should not be drawn between them. For instance, the creation exists as a gift from God as the given and sustaining form of life itself for all humankind. As such, however, its potential as gift is not wholly realized, for it does not yet serve humanity's spiritual life either in a natural or supernatural sense. The fulfillment of the creation as gift, then, goes hand in hand with humanity's fulfillment, one which comprehends its spiritual capacities as well as its material needs and potentials. This fulfillment is, in the end, God's union with the creature so that the creature itself is transparent to God and God transparent through it. The creation relies upon personal human agency as the means by which it is brought into the dialogue of love between humankind and God. That dialogue, Christians believe, is renewed by Christ as part of his renewal of humankind, and participation in that dialogue is a chief manifestation of his risen life in human experience. This is itself a foretaste of the end when creation, together with humankind, is fulfilled in the kingdom. Transparency will reign and 'night will be no more' (Rev. 22.5). 'Nothing will be opaque anymore', says Stăniloae. 'Everything will become transparent; or, put otherwise, Christ himself will become transparent through all things.'[27] 'The whole creation', he goes on, 'will then attain to the final degree of its sacramental destiny.' Its destiny is that it become a 'transparent' and 'communicating' medium of God, a sacrament of supreme transparency, a supreme medium of the communication of Christ's life, power and love.[28]

The transparency which will suffuse the creation perfected as gift at the end of time is distinct from the continued opaqueness of the creation now, and different even from its higher sacramental use. That reflects the tension between faith and sight which characterizes the experience of the believer. The stance of faith is required now so that believers may have a clearer vision. The sacramental life, the sacramental vision, is an experience of a kind of transparency of creation even while it remains opaque. Creation is not transparent to God as gift by

[27] Ibid., 14.
[28] Ibid.

sight; nevertheless, it is by faith, and chiefly in its sacramental form. The sacramental Body of Christ is the point within the created order where that tension is most sharp. The eucharist above all, but the other mysteries too, can be said to occupy an intermediate position between the risen and transparent body of Christ, as known by sight, on the one hand, and that same body discerned by faith through the dialogue of the gift.

Sacramental life then takes a key part in our spiritual growth. It evokes a true sense of God's activity in and relationship to the world. Maximus the Confessor sees that as the second stage of a Christian's spiritual development. In Stăniloae's thought, as in that of Maximus, there is in this way an entrance into the 'epiphanic' quality of creation.[29]

A Three-fold Priesthood

Within this movement of persons and the creation from opaqueness to transparency Stăniloae develops a comple-mentary understanding of priesthood which accords with different stages of that movement. An earlier chapter spoke of the natural priesthood of humanity. The phrase was used to describe humanity's God-given call to use the creation as a gift by offering it back to God in love so that it might become a transparent means of personal communication and com-munion. That natural priesthood was rendered ineffectual by the Fall. We then saw how Christ re-establishes humankind's priestly capacity: through his self-giving, consummated on the cross, the false ultimacy and the opaqueness of the material world is broken. The orientation of matter and spirit Godward become possible again. The transparency of God through the created order is accomplished in Jesus Christ and actualized in history by the Spirit.

Within such a scheme we would expect Stăniloae to attribute to believers as a whole a renewed priestly role. In fact, Stăniloae sees the sacramental life, and the eucharist above all, as the

---

[29] William B. Green describes Maximus's view in 'Maximus confessor: An Introduction', in *Spirit and Light. Essays in Historical Theology*, edd. William B. Green and Madeleine L'Engle (New York, 1976), p. 92.

expression of humanity's renewed capacity to act as priests of creation.[30] As an act of faith the eucharist is both sign and means of humanity's priestly power. He criticizes the West for ignoring the inalienable role of the priesthood of the baptized. Protestantism, he maintains, asserts a common priesthood which consecrates nothing; Catholicism, for its part, asserts a ministerial priesthood which alone consecrates everything.

By contrast, Stăniloae explains, Orthodoxy affirms what he calls a common priesthood of the laity. This priesthood fulfils the half-hearted natural priesthood which men and women, as 'priests of the natural order', exercise in their day to day material sharing. It is the renewed spiritual capacity restored to humanity through consecration in baptism.[31] It reintroduces into the natural priesthood its spiritual and Godward dimension by contact with the mystical Body of Christ. Without this intermediate priesthood, says Stăniloae, there can be only a strict separation between sacred and profane. 'For the theology of western Christianity there is no place for the passage from the order of nature to the order of sacrament.'[32] 'For Eastern theological thought,' he goes on,

> the fact that believers have become members of Christ through Baptism and through other preceding forms of sharing, gives to them the power to bring their gifts to a place, and through them to give themselves to Christ through the priest *completing* this offering. . . . The gifts brought by believers, members of the community of Christ's body, have a status which *anticipates* the transformed gifts. They are no longer exclusively 'natural' when they are brought by the community of the faithful, as they would be when offered by someone in the merely natural order.[33]

Stăniloae is keen to stress that believers are already co-workers with God in the transformation of the world. Through their engagement with the world precisely as believers, using the

---

[30] See my article exploring this theme, 'Presentation of the Gifts: Orthodox Insights for Western Liturgical Renewal,' *Worship*, 60, no. 1 (January, 1986): 27–37.

[31] The Romanian word for 'layman,' *mirean*, or 'anointed one', indicates in part the priestly role of the baptized. See his discussion in *DT*, III, pp. 153–157.

[32] 'Creation,' 19.

[33] Ibid., 20; italics mine.

world for greater solidarity with God and with one another, they renew the world and life itself as gift. In the case of the eucharist the bread and wine brought forth by the faithful occupy a place 'between'. 'They are offered by the mystical Body to its Head in order to become the personal body and blood and of Christ, so that the mystical Body may be nourished by them.'[34] At this point Stăniloae asserts a distinct and necessary role to the ministerial priesthood. He describes its sacramental ministry as 'completing' the common priestly offering of the baptized by explicit invocation of the Spirit, by explicitly drawing the creative gifts into the moment of Christ's cross and resurrection.[35]

Through application of Maximus's notion of the *logos*, understood here as the foundational ontological structure of something, Stăniloae sees all created *logoi* as capable of alteration, expansion, union, incorporation. This capacity is part of what an earlier chapter described as the 'plasticity' of the created order.[36] In regard to the eucharistic gifts Stăniloae sees the change, or better, the expansion of the *logoi* of the bread and wine into the personal body of Christ beginning through contact with the *logoi* of the faithful whose own ontological structure has itself been changed, expanded, through incorporation into Christ's mystical Body, the church. He puts it like this: the foundational or ontological structure [*raţiune ontologica*] of the elements 'is penetrated by the ontological structure of believers, the ecclesial community, which, at its own foundation, is penetrated by Christ himself, the structure behind all structures.'[37] Believers' prior sharing in Christ's body and blood sacramentally means, according to Stăniloae, that they have already become rooted in his uncreated foundation, the divine *Logos*; therefore they are already formed into a 'symphonic, dialogic unity' between creature and Creator. They have progressed toward fulfillment through their return to their source, the creative and unifying Word.

---

[34] Ibid.
[35] Ibid., 19.
[36] See above, pp. 60–62.
[37] 'Creation,' 21.

The 'Third Mystery'

In the *Dogmatic Theology* and in the article from which we have been quoting Stăniloae's discussion of the eucharist leads naturally to a consideration of the church. Those who are familiar with trends in twentieth-century Orthodox theology will not be surprised by the link between the eucharist and the church. It has been one of the most creative areas of Orthodox reflection, and one which western theologians also have found both challenging and fruitful. The precise lines of influence in the case of Stăniloae's thought are not clear. Whatever its relation to wider Orthodox reflection may be, his view of the link between the eucharist and the church is well integrated within his theological vision. It follows from his view of the sacraments which, as we have seen, stresses the context of personal encounter and interaction in faith. Beyond that, however, it is guided by the same two foundational themes which have been discussed in relation to the eucharist itself: Maximus's notion of 'mystery' and the theme of creation as gift.

In building the link between the church and the eucharist along lines inspired by Maximus, Stăniloae speaks of the church as a 'mystery'. Out of the 'new Mystery' or sacrament which is Christ himself, he says, the 'third Mystery,' namely the church, arises.[38] Whereas in the mystery of Christ creatureliness becomes the arena of unity between human persons and the infinite Personal Word who has become incarnate, in the church that same mystery is continued, extended and deepened. 'The actualization of this unity of Christ in an ineffable potential measure with human subjects takes the form of the Church'. 'Thus,' he explains, 'the Church is a kind of third mystery in which God the Word re-establishes and raises to a more accentuated degree his unity with the world, a unity as yet incomplete through the act of creation and weakened by the sin of humankind.'[39]

We can see here why Stăniloae views the church as an 'extension' of the mystery of Christ.[40] That is not so in the sense

[38] *DT*, III, p. 13.
[39] Ibid.
[40] Ibid.

of a replacement for Christ but as an *actualization* (to use a favourite Stăniloae word) of the potential for perfected union which the Incarnation has initiated. Therefore, the church presupposes the first mystery, creation, and the new mystery, Christ. It exists as a third, intermediate mystery in which the other two interact according to God's redemptive purposes.

Eucharist and Church

What, then, is the relationship between the eucharistic mystery and the church? In what sense might Stăniloae say that 'the eucharist makes the church'?[41] A tension always exists, of course, between the church as an institution with a given sacramental structure and the mystery to which it is called to bear witness. It is, in other words, always possible to say at one and the same time that the church already exists and yet is always coming into being. Stăniloae speaks of the 'general' character of the church which is 'actualized' through the sacraments or mysteries.[42]

The chief moment of that actualization is the eucharist. This is because the eucharist above all expresses and actualizes the mystery of Christ. Our earlier discussion of the eucharist spoke of the ontological bond between Christ and believers through the medium of his sacramental body and blood. The direction of Stăniloae's thought leads him to assert that the sacramental body represents the natural order 'raised to supreme transparence, or to the state of a gift which is wholly see-through;' the elements anticipate a creation destined for 'full and all-encompassing transparence to God.'[43]

When the discussion turns to ecclesiology the emphasis shifts to the theme of gift. The focus is no longer a metaphysical structure which allows for the fact of sacraments. Rather, it is the dynamic of gift-giving which, in the milieu of faith, both

---

[41] The phrase of Roman Catholic Henri de Lubac and Orthodox John Zizioulas has been given currency by Fr. Paul McPartlan in his important study *The Eucharist Makes the Church: Henri de Lubac and John Zizioulas In Dialogue* (Edinburgh, 1993).

[42] 'Mystery,' p. 57.

[43] 'Creation,' 14–15.

leads the church to be eucharistic in the first place, and to become the authentic expression of that eucharistic life.

The role of the eucharist in making the church arises from the act of the incarnate and risen Word who *gives himself* in the eucharist. The eucharist, as an enactment of the dialogue of the gift, has its source in Christ, who has become God the Father's perfect gift to us. Christ's existence as perfect gift goes hand in hand with the fact that his sacramental body is wholly trans-parent to God the Giver. The divine perfection conferred by Christ's continuing sacramental presence, is given to us in order that God's character as Giver, who gives to us in the perfect gift, Jesus Christ, might characterize us too. Since by faith we discern God as the 'prime Giver,' Stăniloae explains, Christians are to become 'secondary givers'.[44] The eucharist enables this. This is what Stăniloae means when he says that the church is 'eucharistically determined.' Its eucharistic life, focused in the sacramental presence of him who gave himself – and gives himself – to humankind, becomes the source of giving and sacrifice. The people's giving of bread and wine is a tangible expression of this giving, our opening utterance, as it were, in the renewed dialogue of the gift. In this the givers give themselves to Christ. He then gives himself sacramentally to them so that they may share in 'the perfecting force of the perfected humanity of Christ'.[45] They in turn step toward greater participants in Christ as 'secondary givers,' as more active participants in the dialogue of the gift. That dialogic life forms the church. Stăniloae explains:

> The Church takes shape as a body formed from believers to whom Christ gives himself fully in the Eucharist. Then they, through the power Christ gives of himself, give themselves to one another in a movement of continual convergence and unification . . . The Church is impregnated with the Body of Christ in this movement of His self-giving and in the unification of all both with Him and with one another.[46]

---

[44] Ibid., 24.
[45] Ibid., 26.
[46] Ibid., 18.

As in the eucharist itself this dialogue of the gift, this movement of self-giving, begins with the material creation, the bread and the wine fashioned by believers for believers. It is, at the outset anyway, an exterior act. But as Stăniloae makes clear, it does not stay at that level. The liturgical movement fosters a movement from an act and disposition of exterior gift-giving, the giving of some*thing*, to the giving of some*one*. 'In everything the tendency to give oneself as person is made manifest, to go beyond what one gives or does into a direct union'.[47] In the sacrament itself the some*one* is Christ; yet equally, Christ includes all who by baptism and faith are in him. Thus the giving between Christ and a believer extends to all other believers.

From Sacrament to Solidarity

This dialogue of love believers learn from Christ and express through the eucharist. Likewise, the world is to learn this dialogue of love from believers, Christ's continuing mystical Body in the world. The reality of the sacramental Body is to be the reality of the mystical Body. Yet in living out the dialogue of the gift believers witness not to an arbitrary way of being but rather, Stăniloae insists, to what being human really means: 'The offspring of Adam are made for communion, for a life in the spirit of sacrifice and giving, for life in a eucharistic spirit'. As a corollary, he explains, Christians, acting in the spirit and power of Christ, are called to help others actualize this natural disposition; they are called to help extend this eucharistic spirit of generosity and sacrifice.[48] Eucharistic life is therefore an affirmation of being itself insofar as being human is defined as seeking to give oneself to others. 'In framing oneself freely by the needs of others, as if they were one's own needs, plenitude is realized in the picture frame of one's own life. No one is lost or impoverished but each one is realized and enriched in union with the other in activity and suffering for the other.'[49] To the

---

[47] Ibid., 23.
[48] Ibid., 24–25.
[49] Ibid., 25.

extent that this is so, it makes of the church a 'laboratory' in which God prepares people for, and draws people toward, resurrection life. As a result of its eucharistic centre, says Stăniloae, the church is 'a place in which we are brought back to the forward movement which is proper to our nature'.[50]

But Stăniloae insists that this rediscovery of that being which is proper to humankind is not to be restricted to the faithful. The eucharistic impulse involves for Stăniloae what I would call a movement from sacrament to solidarity. In that movement the gift-giving which believers have learned from Christ and have nurtured among themselves is extended toward those who do not believe, toward the world. That outward movement from the mystery of Christ at the heart of the church is, equally, a movement back to Christ who is the Alpha and Omega of all that is. In opening the world to its full potential as a completely transparent means of communion with God believers draw the eucharist into the world and the world into the eucharist.[51] In so doing, the boundaries of the church itself are enlarged so that, in the end, the whole universe will itself become a unified Holy Mystery, an aspect of the 'third mystery' of the church, a milieu of clear and unhindered communion with God, a eucharistic celebration no longer experienced by faith but by sight, no longer restricted to particular times and places but embracing all time, all space. The gifts of bread and wine, indeed the gift of ourselves, will, by the transfiguring Spirit, include the whole of a transformed and transfigured humanity and creation.

---

[50] 'Mystery,' p. 53.
[51] 'Creation,' 28.

Appendix

The schema of the three volumes of the Romanian edition of the *Orthodox Dogmatic Theology* is as follows:

VOLUME 1

INTRODUCTION

Divine Revelation, the source of Christian faith. The Church, organ and medium of the preservation and fructification of the content of Revelation.

III THE WORK OF CHRIST AND THE HOLY SPIRIT IN PRESERVING THE
     REVELATION'S EFFICACY THROUGH HOLY SCRIPTURE AND HOLY
     TRADITION WITHIN THE FRAMEWORK OF THE CHURCH

A *Means whereby the supernatural Revelation is preserved*
   1. Holy Scripture and its bond with the Church
       through Tradition
   2. Holy Tradition and its bond with the Church and
       Scripture

B *The Church, organ of the Revelation's preservation and
   fruitfulness*
   1. The Church, organ of the Revelation's
       preservation
   2. Dogmas: doctrinal expressions of the plan of
       salvation revealed and realized by God in
       Christ, extended and fructified through the
       Church
   3. Theology: the Church's service of explicating
       and penetrating the dogmas, or the plan of
       salvation, and of vivifying the Church's work of
       service

PART ONE

The Orthodox Christian Teaching

I THREE WAYS OF KNOWING GOD AND HIS ATTRIBUTES

A *The rational and the apophatic knowledge of God*
   1. The inseparability of the rational and the
       apophatic knowledge of God
   2. The distinction between rational and apophatic
       knowledge
   3. The dynamic character of the knowledge of God
       and the transparency of every conception of God

B *The knowledge of God in the concrete surroundings of
   existence*

II THE BEING AND ATTRIBUTES OF GOD

    A The attributes and uncreated energies of God generally

        1. God communicates himself to us through His uncreated energies

        2. The meaning of the character of the divine attributes 'in themselves' and the superexistence of God

        3. The apophatic character of God as superexistent personal reality

    B The attributes in connection with the superexistence of God and creatures' participation in them

        1. The infinity of God and the participation of limited creatures in it

        2. The simplicity or unity of God and the participation in it by composite creatures

        3. The eternity of God; time as the interval between God and the creature, and as the medium of the creature's growth toward participation in His eternity

        4. The superspaciality of God and the creatures' participation in it

        5. The omnipotence of God and the various powers of its effects owing to participation in it

    C The attributes of God in relation to his spiritual nature, and the participation of the creature in them

        1. The omniscience and wisdom of God and participation in it by rational creatures

        2. The judgment and mercy of God

        3. The holiness of God and our participation in it

        4. The goodness and love of God and our participation in them

III THE HOLY TRINITY, STRUCTURE OF SUPREME LOVE

    A The mystery of the Holy Trinity generally

        1. The implication of the Holy Trinity with respect to divine love

B *Man's salvation in the Church; its meanings, phases and conditions*

   1. The means of salvation
   2. The phases or steps of salvation
   3. The necessity of faith and good works for salvation

VOLUME 3

PART FIVE

I THE HOLY MYSTERIES IN GENERAL. THE NOTION OF THE HOLY MYSTERIES

   1. The created components of the Holy Mysteries
   2. The christological and ecclesiological basis of the Mysteries

II PARTICULAR HOLY MYSTERIES

A *The Mystery of Holy Baptism*

   1. The union of water and the Holy Spirit as a sign of the new man
   2. The multiple effects of the act of Baptism and of the declarations made by the priest
   3. The absolute necessity of Baptism for salvation, and the Baptism of children

B *The Mystery of Chrismation*

   1. The connection between the Mystery of Baptism and Chrismation
   2. The significance of the visual act of Chrismation

C *The Divine Eucharist*

   1. The connection between these three Mysteries of Initiation
   2. The real presence of the body and blood of the Lord in the Eucharist and the transformation of the bread and wine

3. The Eucharist as Sacrifice and as Mystery
4. The priest as the one who performs the Eucharist

D *The Mystery of Confession*

1. The institution of the Mystery and its practice from the Church's beginnings
2. The constituent elements and phases of the Mystery

E *The Mystery of Ordination*

1. The difference between ordination and the other sacraments
2. The invisible priesthood of Christ, the source of the visible priesthood of the Church
3. The priesthood and the unity of the Church
4. The institution of the priesthood, and the existence of three kinds of priesthood from the Church's beginning
5. The spiritual character of Christian priestly service and priesthood generally
6. The apostolic succession
7. The visible aspects of ordination and the invisible powers it confers

F *The Mystery of Marriage*

1. The place of Marriage among the other Mysteries
2. Marriage as the natural bond in life between male and female
3. Christ's confirmation and exaltation of Marriage
4. Constituent aspects of the Mystery and their significance for the spiritual power they confer

G *The Mystery of Anointing*

1. The definition and principal purpose of the Mystery
2. Its secondary purposes

PART SIX

Eschatology or the life to come. The perfection of earthly life and eternal life.

I PARTICULAR ASPECTS OF ESCHATOLOGY

   A *Death as the passing from temporal life to eternal life*

   B *The immortality of the souls*

   C *The judgment of the individual and its consequences in regard to the condition of souls*
  1. The necessity of the judgment of the individual
  2. The essence of damnation and the possibility of eternal damnation
  3. The author and criterion of the judgment of individuals
  4. Witnesses, accusers and defenders at the individual's judgment
  5. The status of souls between the individual's judgment and the universal judgment

II UNIVERSAL ESCHATOLOGY

   A *The end of the actual form of the world and its perfection*
  1. The progression of creation to its end
  2. Interpretations of the end of the world as the conclusion of history in its totality
  3. The theory of the eschaton within the confines of history
  4. Conjectures about the condition of the world at the moment of the end
  5. Signs of the end; the invisible cause of the end of the world

   B *The new form of the world, and the manner of progress from its actual to its new form*
  1. The coming of Christ: the cause of the world's transformation and of the resurrection of the dead

Select Bibliography of
Fr. Stăniloae's Writings

Primary Sources in English

'Some Characteristics of Orthodoxy.' *Sobornost*, series 5, no. 9 (1969): 627–629.

'The Orthodox Conception of Tradition and the Development of Doctrine.' *Sobornost*, series 5, no. 9 (1969): 652–662.

'The World as Gift and Sacrament of God's Love.' *Sobornost*, series 5, no. 9 (1969): 662–673.

The Victory of the Cross (Oxford, 1970).

'St. Callinicus of Cernica.' In *The Tradition of Life: Romanian Essays in Spirituality and Theology.* Edited by A. M. Allchin. Studies Supplementary to *Sobornost*, no. 2 (1971): 17–32.

'The Foundation of Christian Responsibility in the World: The Dialogue of God with Man,' In *The Tradition of Life: Romanian Essays in Spirituality and Theology.* Edited by A. M. Allchin. Studies Supplementary to *Sobornost*, no. 2 (1971): 53–73.

'Unity and Diversity in Orthodox Tradition.' *The Greek Orthodox Theological Review*, vol. 17, no. 1 (1972): 19–40.

'Orthodoxy and the World; An Orthodox Comment.' *Sobornost*, series 6, no. 5 (Summer, 1972): 297–300.

'Jesus Christ, Incarnate Logos of God, Source of Freedom and Unity.' *The Ecumenical Review*, vol. 26, no. 3 (1974): 403–412.

'The Role of the Holy Spirit in the Theology and Life of the Orthodox Church.' *Diakonia*, vol. 9, no. 4 (1974): 343–366.

'Romanian Orthodox – Anglican Talks: a Dogmatic Assessment.' In *Romanian Orthodox Church and the Church of England* (Bucharest, 1976): 129–148.

'The Cross in Orthodox Theology and Worship.' *Sobornost*, series 7, no. 4 (1977): 233–243.

Theology and the Church. Translated by Robert Barringer (Crestwood, 1980).

'Witness Through "Holiness" of Life.' In *Martyria—Mission: The Witness of the Orthodox Churches Today*. Edited by Ion Bria (Geneva, 1980): 45–51.

'The Procession of the Holy Spirit from the Fathers and His Relation to the Son, as the Basis of our Deification and Adoption.' In *Spirit of God, Spirit of Christ. Ecumenical Reflections on the Filioque Controversy*, Faith and Order Paper, no. 103 (London: SPCK and Geneva: WCC, 1981): 174–186.

Prayer and Holiness (Oxford, 1982).

'Dumitru Stăniloae' [Interview]. *The Living Church* (17 April 1983): 9–11.

'The Glory of the Lamb.' *The Living Church* (17 April 1983): 8.

'The Mystery of the Church.' In *Church Kingdom World. The Church as Mystery and Prophetic Sign*. Faith and Order Paper, no. 130. Edited by Gennadios Limouris (Geneva, 1986): 50–57.

'Image, likeness, and deification in the human person.' *Communio*, vol. 13, no. 1 (1986): 64–83.

Secondary Sources in English

BARTOS, EMIL *Deification in Eastern Orthodox Thought. An Evaluation and Critique of the Theology of Dumitru Staniloae* (Carlisle, 1999).

BRIA, ION 'A Look at Contemporary Romanian Dogmatic Theology.' *Sobornost*, series 6, no. 5 (1972): 330–336.

BRIA, ION 'The Creative Vision of D. Stăniloae: an Introduction to his Theological Thought.' *The Ecumenical Review*, vol. 33, no. 1 (January, 1981): 53–59.

JUHASZ, ISTVAN 'Dumitru Stăniloae's Ecumenical Studies as an Aspect of Orthodox–Protestant Dialogue.' *Journal of Ecumenical Studies*, vol. 16, no. 4 (1979): 747–764.

MEYENDORFF, JOHN Foreword to Dumitru Stăniloae, *Theology and the Church*. Translated by Robert Barringer (Crestwood, 1980) 7–9.

MILLER, E. C. 'Presentation of the Gifts: Orthodox Insights for Western Liturgical Renewal.' *Worship*, vol. 60, no. 1 (January, 1986): 22–38.

NEESER, DANIEL 'The World: Gift of God and Scene of Humanity's Response: Aspects of the Thought of Father D. Staniloae.' *The Ecumenical Review*, vol. 33, no. 3 (1981): 272–282.

PLĂMĂDEALĂ, ANTONIE 'Some Lines on Professor Staniloae's Theology.' *The Altar* [Bulletin of the Romanian Parish] (London, 1970) 24–29.

Frequently Cited Literature

Where a short title has been used, this is shown at the end of the entry.

ALLCHIN, A. M. 'Dumitru Stăniloae' *Sobornost/ECR* 16:1 (1994).

BEAUREGARD, M.-A. Costa de – *Dumitru Stăniloae: Ose comprendre que Je t'aime* (Paris, 1983).

BRIA, ION 'A Look at Contemporary Romanian Dogmatic Theology' *Sobornost*, series 6, no. 5 (1972): 330–336 (Dogmatic Theology).

——. 'The Creative vision of D. Stăniloae', *The Ecumenical Review*, vol. 33, no. 1 (January, 1987): 53–59 (Vision).

CLÉMENT, OLIVIER Preface to the French translation of the *Orthodox Dogmatic Theology, Le génie de l'Orthodoxie* (Paris, 1985).

GEORGESCU, VLAD *The Romanians, A History* ed. Matei Calinescu (Columbus, 1991).

LOUTH, ANDREW *Discerning the Mystery* (Oxford, 1983).

McGRATH, ALISTER *Luther's Theology of the Cross* (Oxford, 1985) (Cross).

Stăniloae, Dumitru 'Creaţia ca Dar şi Tainele Bisericii [The Creation as Gift and the Mysteries of the Church] *Ortodoxia*, vol. 28, no. 1 (January – March 1976) trans. C. Miller (Creation).

——. *Teologia Dogmatică Ortodoxă*, 3 vols. (Bucharest, 1978) (*DT*).

——. *The Experience of God*, trans. and ed. Ioan Ionita and Robert Barringer (Brookline, 1994) = Vol. 1 of Orthodox Dogmatic Theology (Experience).

——. 'The Mystery of the Church' in *Church, Kingdom, World*, Faith and Order Paper, no. 130 (Geneva, 1986) (Mystery).

——. *Prayer and Holiness* (Oxford, 1982) (Prayer).

——. *The Victory of the Cross* (Oxford, 1970) (Victory).

——. *Theology and the Church*, trans. R. Barringer (Crestwood, 1980)

Thunberg, Lars *Microcosm and Mediator: The theological anthropology of St Maximus the Confessor* (Lund, 1965).

——. *Man and the Cosmos: The Vision of St Maximus the Confessor* (Crestwood, 1985).

Ware, Kallistos (Timothy) *The Orthodox Church* (Baltimore, 1964).

Index of Subjects

Index of Names